D0870224

CAMPAIGN 272

KURSK 1943

The Northern Front

ROBERT FORCZYK   ILLUSTRATED BY STEVE NOON
                           Series editor Marcus Cowper

First published in Great Britain in 2014 by Osprey Publishing,
PO Box 883, Oxford, OX1 9PL, UK
PO Box 3985, New York, NY 10185-3985, USA
E-mail: info@ospreypublishing.com
© 2014 Osprey Publishing Ltd

OSPREY PUBLISHING IS PART OF THE OSPREY GROUP.

ISBN: 978 1 78200 819 4
PDF e-book ISBN: 978 1 78200 820 0
ePub ISBN: 978 1 78200 821 7

Editorial by Ilios Publishing Ltd, Oxford, UK (www.iliospublishing.com) and Nikolai Bogdanovic
Index by Angela Hall
Typeset in Myriad Pro and Sabon
Maps by Bounford.com
3D bird's-eye views by The Black Spot
Battlescene illustrations by Steve Noon
Originated by PDQ Media, Bungay, UK
Printed in China through Worldprint Ltd.

14 15 16 17 18   10 9 8 7 6 5 4 3 2 1

ARTIST'S NOTE

Readers may care to note that the original paintings from which the colour plates in this book were prepared are available for private sale. The Publishers retain all reproduction copyright whatsoever. The artist can be contacted via the following website:
www.steve-noon.co.uk
The Publishers regret that they can enter into no correspondence upon this matter.

THE WOODLAND TRUST

Osprey Publishing are supporting the Woodland Trust, the UK's leading woodland conservation charity, by funding the dedication of trees.

LIST OF ACRONYMS AND ABBREVIATIONS

AA– anti-aircraft
AK – Armeekorps
AOK – Armeeoberkommando (Army Command)
Arko – Artillerie-Kommandeur
AT – anti-tank
BAK – Bomber Aviation Corps
FEB – Feld-Ersatz Bataillon
Fkl – Funklenk
GA – Guards Army
Gd – Guards
GIAD – Guards Fighter Aviation Division
GShAD – Guards Ground Attack Aviation Division
GTA – Guards Tank Army
HArko – Höherer Artillerie-Kommandeur
HE – high-explosive
HQ – headquarters
IAK – Isrebitelnyi Aviatsionnyi Korpus (Fighter Corps)
JG – Jagdgeschwader
KG – Kampfgeschwader
KwK – Kampfwagenkanone
mot. – motorized
MRL – multiple rocket launcher
NAGr – Nahaufklärungsgruppe
NCO – non-commissioned officer
NKVD – Narodnyy Komissariat Vnutrennikh Del (People's Commissariat for Internal Affairs)
OKH – Oberkommando des Heeres
OKL – Oberkommando der Luftwaffe
POZ – podvishnyi otriad zagrazhdenii (mobile obstacle detachments)
PTAB – Protivotankovaya Aviabomba
PzAbt – Panzer-Abteilung
PzAOK – Panzerarmee
PzGren – panzergrenadier
PzK – Panzerkorps
PzKpfw – Panzerkampfwagen
RSO – Raupenschlepper Ost (tractor)
SAK – Composite Air Corps
SchG – Schlachtgeschwader
SdKfz –Sonderkraftfahrzeug
ShAD – Ground Attack Aviation Division
SPW – Schützenpanzerwagen
sPzAbt – schwere Panzer-Abteilung
sPzJgAbt – schwere Panzerjäger-Abteilung
StG – Sturzkampfgeschwader
StuG – Sturmgeschütz
StuGAbt – Sturmgeschütz-Abteliung
StuH – Sturmhaubitze
StuK – Sturmkanone
TA– Tank Army
TSAP – Heavy Self-Propelled Artillery Regiment
VA – Vozdushnaya Armiya (Air Army)
VS – Verbrauchssatz
VVS – Voyenno-Vozdushnye Sily (Military Air Forces)
WIA – wounded in action
ZG – Zerstörergeschwader

Key to military symbols

Key to unit identification

CONTENTS

ORIGINS OF THE CAMPAIGN

The German Army in Russia barely survived the Soviet winter counter-offensive of 1942/43. Even Heeresgruppe Mitte was hard pressed by Soviet offensives at Rzhev and near Orel. Hitler was concerned that the catastrophe at Stalingrad would cause German soldiers to doubt their leaders, and he was desperate to obtain an operational victory in the summer of 1943 to restore frontline morale. (Ian Barter)

After the crippling losses suffered during Operation *Barbarossa* and the subsequent Soviet winter counter-offensive, the German Army succeeded in rebuilding its shattered armoured forces by mid-1942, albeit at great cost. Hitler, always a gambler when it came to strategic decisions, decided to launch a new summer offensive in the southern Soviet Union to seize the oilfields of the Caucasus and to reach the river Volga. Yet in order to assemble the forces for this new offensive, designated *Fall Blau* (Case Blue), Hitler had to strip equipment and personnel from the two non-involved army groups, Heeresgruppe Nord and Heeresgruppe Mitte, to build up Heeresgruppe Süd. In particular, the panzer divisions in Heeresgruppe Mitte were reduced to only a single Panzer-Abteilung (battalion) each, equipped mostly with older models. All new tank production was diverted to re-equip the depleted panzer units in Heeresgruppe Süd. By the time *Fall Blau* began on 28 June 1942, Heeresgruppe Süd had been provided with 70 per-cent of Germany's armour on the Eastern Front, including 32 of Panzer-Abteilung 46 and 13 of Sturmgeschütz-Abteilung 21.

Hitler weighted the forces deployed in the south to increase the likelihood of a successful offensive; however, this also increased the risk in the event of failure. Thus, when Armeeoberkommando (AOK) 6 and part of 4.Panzerarmee were encircled at Stalingrad by the Soviet counter-offensive in November 1942, the ensuing catastrophe affected all German forces on the Eastern Front. At Stalingrad, the Wehrmacht lost 6 of its 25 motorized divisions and 12 of its Panzer-Abteilungen.

After AOK 6 was encircled at Stalingrad, the Red Army launched a series of powerful counter-offensives that pushed Heeresgruppe Süd back all along the line and forced the Germans to abort their campaign in the Caucasus. By February 1943 Soviet armour had liberated Kharkov and was approaching Dnepropetrovsk. For a moment, the German position in southern Ukraine was on the verge of complete collapse. However, the Soviets narrowly failed to finish off Heeresgruppe Süd. Generalfeldmarschall Erich von Manstein was able to mount a desperate counterattack that recaptured Kharkov on 14 March 1943 and brought the Soviet advance to an ignominious halt. Nevertheless, the Soviets were left in possession of the Kursk salient, which protruded into the boundary between Heeresgruppe Mitte and Heeresgruppe Süd. By late March 1943 an unusual lull settled over the area around the Kursk salient.

While the Germans had committed the bulk of their armour in the south in 1942, the Red Army retained significant armoured units around Moscow. Georgy Zhukov, the deputy commander-in-chief of the Red Army, decided to use them against the weakened German Heeresgruppe Mitte. Zhukov believed that a powerful armoured drive towards Orel would divert German reserves from their operations in the south. On 5 July 1942 the Soviet Western Front attacked 2.Panzerarmee's frontline north of Orel on two separate axes – at Zhizdra and Bolkhov. Although the Soviet armour outnumbered the German armour 3:1, 2.Panzerarmee not only stopped the Soviet offensive, but also launched a counter-offensive named *Wirbelwind* that pushed the Soviets back. Zhukov made a second effort against 2.Panzerarmee in late August 1942 and even committed the newly formed 3rd Tank Army (3TA) to create a breakthrough. Nevertheless, the Germans succeeded in stopping the Western Front offensive and 3TA lost 500 of its 700 tanks. The tank battles north of Orel in July and August 1942 were some of the largest armoured engagements of the year, but they remain little known today.

Zhukov also made an effort to cut off Generaloberst Walter Model's AOK 9 (9th Army) in the Rzhev salient, by massing over 2,300 tanks against the base of the salient. However, when Operation *Mars* was launched on 25 November 1942, it proved to be a fiasco that cost Zhukov's forces over 1,800 tanks. Model even succeeded in cutting off the Soviet armoured spearheads, thereby destroying two tank and two mechanized corps. Given these successes in 1942, the senior leadership in Heeresgruppe Mitte believed that Soviet numerical superiority could be blunted with superior defensive tactics.

Nevertheless, the long-term forecast for the Wehrmacht on the Eastern Front after Stalingrad looked increasingly bleak. In 1942 the Red Army lost about 20,000 tanks, while Soviet industry built 24,231 tanks and Anglo-American Lend-Lease provided another 10,500 tanks. This meant that the Red Army had experienced a net increase of more than 14,000 tanks by the beginning of 1943. At this point it was decided to phase out the KV-1 heavy tank in favour of producing larger numbers of the reliable T-34/76 medium tank. By July 1943 Soviet industry was manufacturing 1,393 T-34 tanks per month. In contrast, the Wehrmacht lost about 2,480 tanks on the Eastern Front in 1942, plus another 563 tanks in North Africa, while German industry built only 4,168 tanks in 1942. Even after the PzKpfw III had been phased out in early 1943, German tank production remained inadequate, with only 511 tanks being built in July 1943 (of which 244 were PzKpfw IV, 202 were Panthers and 65 were Tigers). Hitler hoped to counter the increasing Soviet numerical superiority in armour by introducing qualitatively superior tanks like the Tiger and Panther, but the diversion of industrial resources to construct these new models hindered increases in the production of the existing PzKpfw IV. By spring 1943 it was evident that the Red Army would enjoy a large numerical superiority in armour for the upcoming summer campaigns. It was questionable whether the Wehrmacht could regain the strategic initiative under these conditions.

Nevertheless, after partially rebuilding Heeresgruppe Süd, Hitler intended to conduct a limited objective offensive in the summer of 1943 to regain the initiative. He also wanted a tangible victory in order to bolster home-front morale and restore confidence within the Wehrmacht. Manstein, optimistic after his 'backhand blow' victory at Kharkov, felt that the Soviet forces in the Kursk salient formed a tempting target. Although German offensive capabilities were much reduced from previous years, the elimination of the Soviet-held Kursk salient by means of a classic combined-arms pincer attack seemed feasible. In fair weather and with air support, this operational method had always worked for the Germans against the Red Army in the past. By encircling the bulk of the Soviet Central and Voronezh fronts in the Kursk salient, Hitler hoped that the resulting heavy losses of troops and materiel inflicted on the Red Army would grant the Wehrmacht sufficient time to recover its strength fully. He was looking for an 'easy victory', not a battle of attrition. However, Hitler had apparently overlooked the fact that similar efforts to encircle large Soviet formations during the opening stages of *Fall Blau* in July and August 1942 had failed to net significant amounts of prisoners. Moreover, Soviet defensive capabilities had improved greatly by early 1943.

A panzer crewman loads ammunition into a PzKpfw IV medium tank in an assembly area located in a village. Heeresgruppe Mitte's panzer divisions had been weakened in 1942 in order to strengthen Heeresgruppe Süd's panzer formations for *Fall Blau* (Case Blue), and were still well below strength when Hitler began planning *Zitadelle* in early 1943. (Ian Barter)

CHRONOLOGY

1943

13 March	Hitler orders the Oberkommando des Heeres (OKH – the Supreme High Command) to begin planning for a summer offensive in Russia.
11 April	The OKH presents the first draft of Operation *Zitadelle* (Citadel) and issues a warning order.
12 April	Stalin authorizes a shift to the strategic defensive in the Kursk salient, in anticipation of the German offensive.
15 April	Operations Order No. 6, for Operation *Zitadelle*, is issued.
4 May	Hitler postpones *Zitadelle* until mid-June.
1 July	Hitler sets 5 July as the start date for *Zitadelle*.
5 July	AOK 9 begins its offensive as part of *Zitadelle*.
6 July	Rokossovsky commits part of the 2nd Tank Army to a counterattack; it fails.
10 July	Although 4.Panzer-Division captures Teploye, AOK 9 suspends its offensive.
12 July	The Western and Bryansk fronts begin Operation *Kutusov*.
14 July	Hitler gives Model authority over 2.Panzerarmee.
15 July	The Central Front joins in Operation *Kutusov*.
19 July	Rybalko's 3rd Guards Tank Army enters the battle.
26 July	Badanov's 4th Guards Tank Army enters the battle; the German Gruppe Harpe abandons Bolkhov.
31 July	Hitler authorizes Model to evacuate the Orel salient.
1 August	Operation *Herbstreise* ('autumn journey' – the evacuation) begins.
5 August	Orel is liberated.
18 August	Operation *Kutusov* ends.

OPPOSING PLANS

GERMAN PLANS

Hitler directed OKH to begin initial planning for Operation *Zitadelle* in early March 1943; Operations Order No. 5 was issued on 13 March 1943 as a warning order for Heeresgruppe Mitte and Heeresgruppe Süd. Hitler chose two of his best field commanders – Generalfeldmarschall Erich von Manstein and Generaloberst Walter Model – to lead the twin pincers of Operation *Zitadelle* against the Kursk salient. Manstein's Heeresgruppe Süd would attack from the south with 4.Panzerarmee while Model attacked from the north with his reinforced AOK 9.

As a necessary prerequisite for *Zitadelle*, Model's AOK 9 successfully evacuated the Rzhev salient with Operation *Buffalo* in early March 1943. This evacuation greatly reduced the amount of frontline that Heeresgruppe Mitte needed to hold, and created a reserve pool of divisions which could be used either for defensive or offensive purposes. Both Model and his superior, Generalfeldmarschall Günther von Kluge, anticipated further major Soviet offensives in the summer of 1943, and wanted to keep these surplus divisions as a ready reserve – but Hitler had no interest in defensive strategies. Instead, Model's AOK 9 headquarters was transferred to Orel and ordered to begin offensive planning. However, only 6 of Model's 22 divisions from AOK 9 were transferred to Orel, with the rest distributed elsewhere within Heeresgruppe Mitte. Further clarification came with OKH Operation Order No. 6 on 15 April 1943, which provided more guidance on operational boundaries and objectives. In the order, Hitler specified that he wanted the offensive to begin 'as soon as the weather permits', and that he wanted 'the best units, the best weapons, the best leaders and great quantities of munitions … to be focused at the *schwerpunkt* [point of main effort]'. Hitler believed that *Zitadelle* would result in the encirclement and destruction of a larger Soviet force than he had lost at Stalingrad, thereby allowing Germany to regain the strategic initiative in the East and for Hitler himself to gain a prestigious victory. Initially, it was expected that the operation would begin in early May 1943.

As part of *Zitadelle*, Model's specified task was to plan and conduct a full-scale offensive to penetrate the northern portion of the Kursk salient by smashing through General Konstantin Rokossovsky's Central Front. However, Model knew that his army was in no shape to conduct a major offensive, since most of his infantry divisions only had between 50 and

The German plan for *Zitadelle*, July 1943.

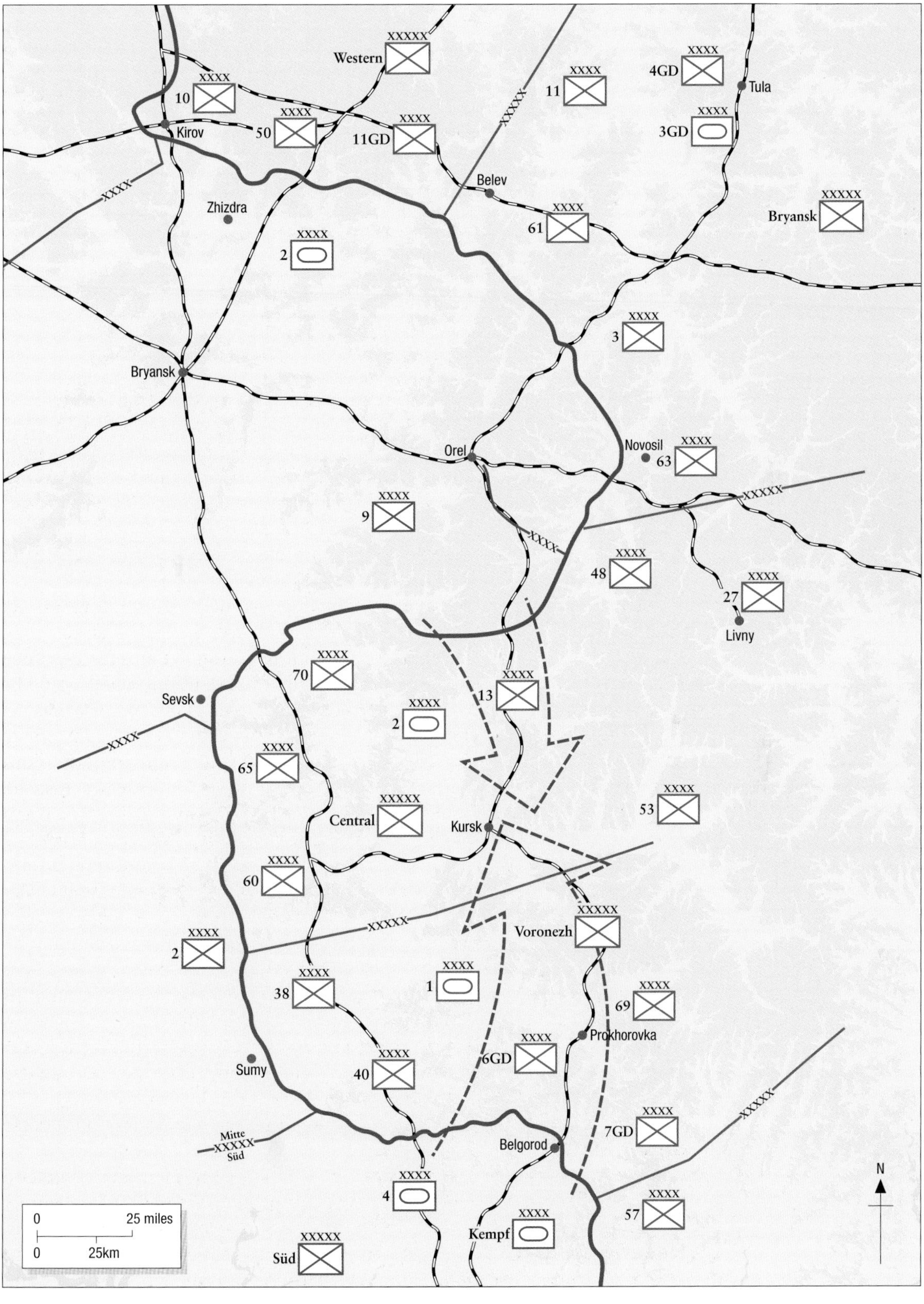

Western

10
Kirov
50
11GD
Belev
Zhizdra
2
61
11
4GD
Tula
3GD
Bryansk

Bryansk
Orel
9
48
3
Novosil
63
27
Livny

70
Sevsk
2
13
65
Central
Kursk
60
53

2
38
1
Voronezh
Sumy
40
6GD
Prokhorovka
69
Mitte
XXXXX
Süd
4
57
Kempf
Belgorod
7GD
Süd

0   25 miles
0   25km

N

60 per-cent of their authorized troop strength, and his panzer units were also depleted. As usual, Hitler promised replacement troops and tanks, but then failed to make good on this. Model also knew that the Soviets were heavily fortifying the Kursk salient, that Rokossovsky's forces had built three lines of defence, and that they outnumbered his own troops by at least 2:1; consequently, he was not sanguine about the prospects for success. Conventional military theory regarded a 3:1 numerical superiority in favour of the attacker as a *sine qua non* for a successful breakthrough against a fortified line. Instead, Model was being ordered to mount a frontal assault against a very strong fortified line with a numerical inferiority in men and tanks. His assessment was that, at best, he would gain some ground, albeit at great cost – precisely what Stavka (the Soviet high command) wanted to occur. Model intended to disappoint them.

Rather unusually for the Wehrmacht, a debate about the efficacy of *Zitadelle* developed between Hitler, the OKH, and senior German field commanders. Manstein was one of the few who argued that not only would the operation succeed, but that it should begin as soon as possible. In his memoirs, he suggested that if the offensive had proceeded as planned in May, the Soviets would have been caught unprepared. This, however, was far from the truth. By mid-May the Red Army fully expected an attack at Kursk and was rapidly fortifying its positions. Generaloberst Heinz Guderian, newly appointed as Inspector of Panzertruppen, was opposed to the offensive and tried to persuade Hitler to cancel it altogether. Model also believed that *Zitadelle* was 'senseless' and would result in 'large losses and no success'. In late April 1943 Model wrote a memorandum to OKH outlining his

The most significant reinforcement that AOK 9 received for *Zitadelle* was schwere Panzer-Abteilung 505 with two companies of Tiger tanks; it arrived by rail at Orel on 6 May 1943. Note the spare track piled in front of the lead Tiger, where the crewmen are standing. The failure to provide this battalion with spare engines, transmissions and roadwheels prior to *Zitadelle* led to most of the Tigers becoming non-operational after just four days of combat. (Ian Barter)

arguments against *Zitadelle*. Furthermore, he later provided Hitler with aerial reconnaissance photos that revealed the Soviets were building multiple lines of defence to protect the base of the Kursk salient, which indicated that strategic surprise was already lost. Model thought that an outright German success was unlikely given the scale of Soviet preparations; even if Kursk could be reached, German losses would be so heavy as to render it a pyrrhic victory. Instead, he argued, AOK 9 should remain on the defensive and allow the Red Army to attack the Orel salient first, so that the panzer reserves could be used to cut off and destroy the Soviet spearheads – just as they had done during Operation *Mars*. However, Kluge, commander of Heeresgruppe Mitte, did not agree with Model's pessimistic assessment and tried to downplay the value of Soviet defensive preparations. Nevertheless, Hitler was sufficiently moved by Model's arguments to agree to delay the offensive until further reinforcements could reach both army groups, although he refrained from cancelling an operation that his subordinate commanders regarded as reckless. Instead, he convinced himself that heavy armoured fighting vehicles like the Tiger and the Ferdinand could break through any resistance. As more German officers criticized *Zitadelle*, Hitler continued to delay the operation throughout June. Finally, on 1 July, he set the start date as 5 July.

Once Hitler's mind was made up, Model began planning his army's part in *Zitadelle*. However, he was unwilling to commit everything he had to this high-risk venture. The *Zitadelle* plan tasked Model's AOK 9 with penetrating the Central Front's three lines of defence and advancing 77km to link up with the spearheads of 4.Panzerarmee in or near Kursk. He intended to attack with four of his corps across a 40km-wide front, with the *schwerpunkt* made in the centre by XXXXI and XXXXVII Panzerkorps. Yet Model knew that even if he breached Rokossovsky's outer defences, he would need at least a dozen divisions to hold the flanks of a narrow penetration corridor all the way to Kursk – which the Soviets could easily lop off with an armoured counterattack. If this occurred, Model would not only lose the bulk of his armour, but also control of the Orel salient – and perhaps even most of AOK 9. He resolved to conserve his panzers as far as possible and to avoid all-or-nothing gambles, despite Hitler's stated intent. German intelligence knew that the Soviet 2nd Tank Army was deployed behind Rokossovsky's outer defences, but was unaware that the 3rd and 4th Guards Tank armies were not far away. Model did not know that he would have to face three Soviet tank armies.

While readying his troops for the offensive, Model also began to make preparations to defend the Orel salient in conjunction with 2.Panzerarmee. Since 2.Panzerarmee had been stripped of most of its armour and artillery to reinforce AOK 9, it would have great difficulty withstanding a new offensive by the Bryansk or Western fronts. Without authorization from Hitler or OKH, Model decided to hedge his bets by quietly directing AOK 9 engineers to begin work on the *Hagen Stellung* (fortified position) at the base of the Orel salient, so that his army would have a position to retreat to in case of a major Soviet counter-offensive. Two panzer units, 5.Panzer-Division and 8.Panzer-Division with a total of 169 tanks, were kept out of *Zitadelle* to defend either side of the base of the Orel salient. Model's contingency planning was in stark contrast to Manstein's unwillingness to make any defensive preparation in the event that *Zitadelle* failed to achieve its objectives. Model regarded the Orel salient as an excellent place to employ Napoleon's 'strategy of the central position', by using interior lines to defeat each attacking Soviet front in turn. However, the trick was in not having to fight all three Soviet fronts simultaneously.

Model's offensive planning for *Zitadelle* appears to have been based upon the concept of inflicting as much damage upon Rokossovsky's Central Front as possible, rather than seizing a great deal of terrain. Model knew that the small town of Ponyri, with a pre-war population about 5,000 and sitting astride the Orel–Kursk rail line, was not an objective worth a great deal of German blood. He also knew that Rokossovsky's troops had owned this terrain for five months; it would be heavily mined and fortified. His concept was to begin his attack primarily with well-supported infantry in order to 'feel out' the Soviet defences and look for weak points, rather than commit all his armour up front as Manstein did with 4.Panzerarmee in *Zitadelle*. The Luftwaffe's 1.Flieger-Division was also ordered to focus all its resources on supporting Model's *schwerpunkt*; no assets were to be used to attack Soviet airfields or to conduct battlefield interdiction. This in itself was a departure from standard German methods, which usually sought to isolate the battlefield. Instead, Model was inviting Rokossovsky to a major clash of armour and airpower over a collection of obscure rural Russian townships, and trusting to superior German tactics to inflict disproportionate losses on the enemy. If Rokossovsky's best forces could be crippled, then Model could pivot to defeat any offensive moves by the Western or Bryansk fronts. However, all Model's planning was based upon the necessity of keeping his options open and retaining sufficient reserves to respond to a Soviet multi-front counter-offensive.

Another important fact that evaded Model was that both the Allies and the Soviets were being kept apprised of the planning for *Zitadelle*. The OKH was using encrypted cipher traffic over teleprinters to communicate orders related to *Zitadelle* to Heeresgruppe Mitte and Heeresgruppe Süd, without realizing that the British had laboriously broken the cipher in 1942. A sub-unit of the Ultra programme, known as 'Tunny', was regularly intercepting and decrypting these German orders by 1943, and the basic outline of *Zitadelle* was passed to the Soviets in a timely manner. On 2 July Stavka was informed that Hitler had made his final decision to attack and that *Zitadelle* would begin in the next several days. Forewarned by 'Tunny', Stavka knew far more about *Zitadelle* than they had about any previous German offensives.

SOVIET PLANS

After the Soviet defeat at Kharkov in mid-March 1943, the onset of spring mud temporarily brought a halt to all operations, giving Stavka time to assess the situation on the Eastern Front. Most senior Soviet officers felt that the Wehrmacht would attempt to mount a counter-offensive in spring 1943; a double envelopment of the Kursk salient was the most likely enemy course of action. Always eager to attack and regain territory, no matter what the cost, Stalin believed that once the Red Army had caught its breath and replaced its losses, it should renew the offensive to destroy Heeresgruppe Süd. However, many officers in Stavka were more cautious after Manstein's 'backhand blow' at Kharkov, and realized that the German Army still posed a significant danger. On 12 April 1943 Deputy Commander-in-Chief Zhukov and Chief of the General Staff Marshal Aleksandr Vasilevsky briefed Stalin on the situation. They both urged caution. Instead, the Red Army should allow the Germans to attack first, since the objective was obvious; the Kursk salient could be heavily fortified to inflict maximum losses on any attackers. By this point Soviet generals had gained much firsthand experience of German tactical and operational methods and knew that any offensive would be spearheaded by panzer divisions supported by ground-attack aircraft. Since the Red Army now had adequate anti-tank weaponry to handle even massed German armour and the *Voyenno-Vozdushnye Sily* (VVS – the Military Air Forces) was strong enough now to contest air superiority over the battlefield, Zhukov argued that the German offensive could be shut down with heavy losses in tanks and aircraft. This would then set the stage for powerful Soviet counter-offensives to throw the disrupted enemy back on their heels. After considerable debate, Stalin was finally persuaded of the military logic of temporarily shifting to a strategic defence, while planning for follow-up counter-offensives.

As a result, Rokossovsky's Central Front was tasked with developing a defence-in-depth of the northern shoulder of the Kursk salient, in order to defeat any effort by Model's AOK 9 to conduct a pincer attack toward Kursk. In April 1943 over 100,000 local civilians were recruited to assist in digging 5,000km of trenches and anti-tank ditches north of Kursk. By June 1943 there were 300,000 people working on this task. Three lines of defence were constructed, with the most effort put into the first line. Thousands of mines were emplaced, beginning with the Outpost Line and extending through the Main Defensive Belts. The Soviets intended to mass their anti-tank guns in areas where they expected the Germans to attack. In conjunction with strong anti-aircraft defences, these so-called 'Pakfronts' were intended to decimate the German armour–air support team. In the 13th Army sector, which was expected to form Model's main avenue of approach, Rokossovsky massed 23 anti-tank guns per kilometre of front – double the density that the Voronezh Front deployed to stop 4.Panzerarmee in the south. Rokossovsky, Zhukov and Vasilevsky all hoped that Model's AOK 9 would impale itself on the hardened

The Soviet decision to fortify the Kursk salient in depth, rather than launch a spring offensive, provided Rokossovsky's Central Front with sufficient time and resources to build a virtually impenetrable defence. Model was aware of the extent of Soviet preparations, but Hitler and other members of OKH refused to believe that the blitzkrieg tactics of 1941–42 would fail to penetrate these defences. (Author's collection)

Soviet defences, with crippling losses in the best panzer and Luftwaffe units. Expecting the Luftwaffe to attack his air bases in the opening stages of *Zitadelle*, General-Leytenant Sergei I. Rudenko's 16th Air Army dispersed his aircraft to multiple airfields, which were ringed with anti-aircraft (AA) guns.

The 'rock' of Rokossovsky's Central Front was General-Leytenant Nikolai P. Pukhov's 13th Army, which held the Ponyri–Maloarkhangel'sk sector with 114,000 troops in 12 divisions. Pukhov was provided with 270 tanks for infantry support, as well as two artillery divisions and two anti-aircraft divisions. Less than 25km to the south, General-Leytenant Aleksei G. Rodin's 2nd Tank Army and the 9th and 19th Independent Tank corps waited in reserve with nearly 800 tanks. Altogether, Rokossovsky had 711,575 troops in his Central Front and enjoyed a 2:1 advantage in manpower and armour against Model's AOK 9. Yet despite the intelligence provided by 'Tunny', Rokossovsky was not sure about exactly when Model's AOK 9 would attack, since *Zitadelle* had been repeatedly postponed. At least he knew where it would hit, which deprived the Germans of their accustomed advantage in operational-level surprise. Under these conditions, Rokossovsky had no doubt that he could stop the German offensive toward Kursk. He developed several variants to his defensive plan, mostly differentiated by where and when he would commit his own armoured reserves to stop Model's offensive.

Once Model's offensive was defeated, Stalin wanted the Western, Bryansk and Central fronts to switch to a counter-offensive within a few days. This counter-offensive, designated Operation *Kutusov*, comprised a simultaneous, multi-front operation that would quickly defeat both 2.Panzerarmee and AOK 9 and liberate the entire Orel salient. Zhukov was sent by Stavka to coordinate the inter-front planning between Rokossovsky, Vasily Sokolovsky's Western Front and Markian Popov's Bryansk Front. Zhukov believed that it would be possible to encircle and destroy most of the German forces in the Orel salient, although the actual *Kutusov* plan was more focused on seizing key objectives, such as Bolkhov and Orel. Even though the three fronts enjoyed a marked superiority over the German forces holding the Orel salient (2.7:1 in manpower, 2.5:1 in armour and more than 4:1 in aircraft), Zhukov regarded the initial defence against AOK 9's attack as a vital prerequisite for the success of *Kutusov*. Yet he knew from his own bitter experience at Rzhev that even a few intact panzer divisions could cause a great deal of trouble for Soviet armoured spearheads.

The main problem for Zhukov was in coordinating superior Soviet resources to achieve decisive results on the battlefield. Model enjoyed the advantage of unity of command and interior lines, whereas Zhukov had great difficulty coordinating the activities of three fronts operating on exterior lines. Model hoped to prevail in a defence of the Orel salient by picking off one opponent at a time, and it was Zhukov's challenge to overwhelm him with simultaneous thrusts. Faced with the difficulty of coordinating with three front commanders, Zhukov opted to keep the best operational reserves under direct Stavka (and thus his personal) control. He allowed the Western and Bryansk fronts to retain their tank brigades and several independent tank corps for infantry support in the breakthrough attacks, but kept the entire 3rd Guards Tank Army, the 4th Tank Army and 11th Army in reserve to use as an exploitation force at the moment he thought best. Zhukov's decision to centrally direct armoured reserves ensured that Soviet mass could be employed at the decisive point, but it also deprived the frontal commanders of the flexibility to use these forces in a timely manner and as they saw fit.

OPPOSING COMMANDERS

GERMAN COMMANDERS

Generaloberst Walter Model (1891–1945)

Model was commissioned as an infantry officer in 1910 and saw extensive frontline service in France during World War I. Afterwards he rose through the post-war Reichswehr and served as a corps-level chief of staff in the French and Polish campaigns. In 1941 Model was given command of 3.Panzer-Division, which he led brilliantly during Operation *Barbarossa*, including directing the pincer that created the Kiev pocket. During Operation *Typhoon*, Model was bumped up to command XXXXI Armeekorps (mot.) and distinguished himself during offensive and defensive combat around Klin. Assigned to take over the crumbling AOK 9 at Rzhev in January 1942, Model pulled off a series of defensive miracles that restored Heeresgruppe Mitte's shattered left flank and helped to frustrate Zhukov's winter counter-offensive. Model was badly wounded in May 1942 but returned later to prevent Zhukov's forces from overrunning the Rzhev salient in August that year. He then inflicted a crushing defeat on the Soviets in Operation *Mars* in November and December 1942.

Model was the best defensive tactician in the German Army, but he was also a proven aggressive commander in the attack. Furthermore, he was one of the very few field commanders who successfully stood up to Hitler, the latter respecting his tough, no-nonsense approach. Model opposed Operation *Zitadelle* as both impractical (given the level of Soviet defences) and a waste of German resources (believing they would be better employed building up a mobile reserve for the Eastern Front). Nevertheless, he obediently executed his phase of the operation to the best of his ability, albeit in a manner that preserved his forces and his options.

Generaloberst Walter Model with his chief of staff Generalleutnant Hans Krebs, making snowballs during the winter of 1942/43. Despite his affected Prussian command style, Model was very much a non-traditional officer. He was known as a 'hard ass' among his staff, but always managed to get the optimum results out of his units. He also maintained excellent situational awareness of what was going on at the front. (Author's collection)

General der Panzertruppen Joachim Lemelsen (1888–1954)

Lemelsen was commissioned as an artillery officer in 1908. He served in World War I and the post-war Reichswehr. At the start of World War II Lemelsen was commanding 29.Infanterie-Division (mot.), which he led in the Polish and French campaigns. He briefly commanded 5.Panzer-Division in the later stages of 1940 campaign, and was then given command of XXXXVII Armeekorps (mot.); he led this unit during *Barbarossa* in 1941 and then (as XXXXVII Panzerkorps) in the defensive battles against the Western Front offensive north of Orel in July and August 1942. During *Zitadelle*, Model believed that Lemelsen disobeyed his orders and did not put enough effort into capturing Ol'khovatka.

General der Panzertruppen Josef Harpe (1887–1968)

Harpe was commissioned into the Prussian Army as an infantry officer in 1911. He served in World War I and was then retained in the post-war Reichswehr. In 1934 he began transitioning to the new motorized forces and took command of Panzer-Regiment 3 in 1935. At the start of World War II Oberst Harpe led Panzer-Brigade 1 in the invasion of Poland. He missed the French campaign due to being put in charge of the Panzertruppenschule in Wünsdorf, but led 12.Panzer-Division during Operation *Barbarossa* in 1941. Harpe's division was defeated at Tikhvin, but he was awarded the Oak Leaves to his *Ritterkreuz* for his role in directing defensive combat. Appointed commander of XXXXI Panzerkorps in January 1942, he led this unit during the short-lived *Wirbelwind* counter-offensive near Bolkhov in August that year, and then scored a major defensive victory against the Kalinin Front at Belyi during Operation *Mars*. Harpe was part of Model's trusted inner circle of competent subordinates.

General der Infanterie Lothar Rendulic (1887–1971)

Rendulic was born in Austria and was commissioned as an infantry officer in the Austro-Hungarian Army in 1910. He briefly served on the Eastern Front as a frontline, company-grade officer in World War I until he was badly wounded in October 1914; thereafter, he was retrained as a general staff officer. After the war Rendulic remained in the Austrian Army, but took time off to obtain a law degree. He joined the Austrian Nazi Party in 1932. When Austria was incorporated into the Reich in 1938, Rendulic switched to the German Army and became chief of staff of XVII Armeekorps in the Polish campaign. His son was killed during the latter. In October 1940 Rendulic was given command of 52.Infanterie-Division, which he led in Russia during 1941 and 1942. He was awarded the

General der Panzertruppen Joachim Lemelsen, commander of XXXXVII Panzerkorps. (Author's collection)

General der Panzertruppen Josef Harpe, commander of XXXXI Panzerkorps. (Author's collection)

Ritterkreuz in March 1942. In November of that year he was appointed commander of XXXV Armeekorps. Rendulic was a tough, smart, well-trained and fanatical opponent.

General der Infanterie Hans Zorn (1891–1943)

Zorn was commissioned as a Bavarian infantry officer in 1911 and saw considerable frontline service on the Western Front in World War I. He commanded 20.Infanterie-Division (mot.) during Operation *Barbarossa* and Operation *Typhoon*. In March 1942 he participated in the relief of the Demyansk pocket. In June 1942 he became commander of XXXXVI Panzerkorps, and took part in the defensive battles around Rzhev between August and December that year. He was killed in an air attack on 2 August 1943 during Operation *Kutusov*.

General der Infanterie Erich-Heinrich Clößner (1888–1976)

Clößner became commander of 2.Panzerarmee in April 1943, taking over Guderian's old command three months prior to *Zitadelle* (Generaloberst Rudolf Schmidt had been relieved of command and narrowly avoided conviction for treason). Clößner had proved himself to be an able commander of LIII Armeekorps but also fell under suspicion from the Gestapo due to anti-regime remarks. He was relieved of command just three days after the start of *Kutusov*. Clößner's deteriorating situation briefly undermined 2.Panzerarmee's command and control, but paved the way for Model to take over all German forces in the Orel salient.

General der Infanterie Lothar Rendulic, commander of XXXV Armeekorps. (Bundesarchiv, Bild 146-1995-027-32A)

SOVIET COMMANDERS

General Konstantin K. Rokossovsky (1896–1968)

Rokossovsky was born in Warsaw and was of mixed Russian–Polish stock. He served in the tsarist cavalry as a non-commissioned officer (NCO) in World War I. Later he joined the Red Army and served as a cavalry officer during the Russian Civil War (1918–21). Rokossovsky rose rapidly in the interwar period, but was arrested during the Stalinist purges in 1937 and held in prison for three years; during this time, all his teeth were smashed out. He was reinstated in early 1940, and at the start of the German invasion he commanded 9th Mechanized Corps during the border battles near Dubno. In September 1941 he was sent to Smolensk, where he attempted to break through the German blocking position at Yartsevo. During the battle of Moscow (October 1941–January 1942), Rokossovsky commanded 16th Army, which conducted a tenacious defence on the approaches to the capital. He fought along the Bryansk sector for much of 1942, but then was sent to command Stalingrad Front during Operation *Uranus*. In February 1943 he

General Konstantin K. Rokossovsky, commander of Central Front. (Author's collection)

General-Leytenant Nikolai P. Pukhov, commander of 13th Army. (Author's collection)

was made commander of Central Front. Rokossovsky was one of the more skilled senior Red Army commanders at this time, capable of orchestrating successful combined-arms offensive and defensive operations. However, he tended towards caution in order to avoid mistakes.

General-Leytenant Nikolai P. Pukhov (1895–1958)

Pukhov served as a junior cavalry officer in the tsarist army during World War I, then transitioned to the infantry branch in the Red Army. He spent a good deal of the 1930s in academic training assignments, but commanded 304th Rifle Division in 1941. He was made commander of 13th Army in January 1942. Prior to the battle of Kursk, he led defensive combat around Voronezh, which gave him some experience in stopping German armour. However, he paid insufficient attention to the defensive preparations of his subordinates, which led to the near collapse of his left flank at the outset of *Zitadelle*. Pukhov remained in command of 13th Army until May 1945, which was highly unusual for a senior Soviet commander. He was solid and reliable, but no more.

General-Leytenant Pavel S. Rybalko (1892–1948)

Rybalko was an experienced armour officer who spent the first year of the Russo-German war far from the front, as an instructor at the Kazan Tank School. Rybalko had an academic mind-set and was a student of armoured doctrines. He was finally given a field command in October 1942, taking over 3rd Guards Tank Army. He led this unit during the 1942/43 winter counter-offensive, but his over-extended forces were defeated by Manstein's 'backhand blow' at Kharkov in March 1943.

General-Leytenant Aleksei G. Rodin (1902–55)

Rodin was a very experienced armour officer, who had led brigades, divisions and corps in battle between 1941 and 1943. During Operation *Uranus* in November 1942 Rodin led the 26th Tank Corps to Kalach, to complete the encirclement of Friedrich Paulus' AOK 6. He was promoted to command of 2nd Tank Army in February 1943. However, he was much less successful in leading this unit during the Sevsk offensive in February and March 1943, failing to break through AOK 2's defences.

General-polkovnik Ivan Khristoforovich Bagramyan (1897–1982)

Born in Armenia, Bagramyan served in the tsarist army during World War I. He then served in the Armenian national army between 1918 and 1920, before joining the Red Army. He moved up slowly in the ranks of the latter's cavalry during the interwar period, but succeeded in developing relationships with upcoming officers such as Zhukov. At the start of the German invasion he was deputy chief of staff for South-West Front and only narrowly avoided being lost in the Kiev encirclement. Thereafter, Bagramyan served in key staff assignments, such as planning the disastrous May 1942 Kharkov counter-offensive. In July 1942 he was given command of 16th Army, and became commander of 11th Guards Army in April 1943.

General-Leytenant Aleksei G. Rodin, commander of 2nd Tank Army. (Author's collection)

General Vasiliy D. Sokolovsky (1897–1968)

Sokolovsky had primarily been a mid-to-high-level staff officer for most of his career in the Red Army, and was a protégé of Georgy Zhukov. As an operational planner, he presided over the failed Zhizdra–Bolkhov offensive in July and August 1942, as well as Operation *Mars* in November 1942 – by no means a stellar record of success. Sokolovsky was more of a resource manager and high-level paper pusher than a battlefield commander. Despite this, he was made commander of Western Front in February 1943. By the middle of that year, the Red Army still only had a handful of really effective front-level commanders and had to make do with a number of mediocre officers like Sokolovsky, who mostly characterized themselves by following orders.

General Vasiliy D. Sokolovsky, commander of Western Front. (Author's collection)

General-polkovnik Markian M. Popov (1902–69)

Popov was a well-regarded officer who had risen quickly in the interwar Red Army. However, he turned in a lacklustre performance at the start of the war. He initially commanded Leningrad Front until relieved in September 1941, then spent the next year-and-a-half in the Bryansk and South-West fronts. His 'Mobile Group Popov' was demolished by Manstein's counter-offensive in March 1943. Zhukov regarded him as intelligent, but (even by Soviet standards) his personal problems – excessive drinking and womanizing – interfered with his military responsibilities. He was made commander of Bryansk Front in June 1943. His battle command during Operation *Kutusov* was mediocre at best.

OPPOSING FORCES

GERMAN

A soldier from 78.Sturm-Division hurls a Stielhandgranaten at the enemy. This elite division failed to accomplish its objectives during *Zitadelle* and suffered almost 2,000 casualties in the process. The quality of German infantry declined rapidly after the bloodletting in the battle of Kursk. (Author's collection)

Since the beginning of the Russo-German war AOK 9 had been an infantry army and was typically assigned defensive missions or supporting attacks. In contrast, 2.Panzerarmee (originally Panzergruppe Guderian) had been an offensive formation. By 1943 roles and missions in the German Army were becoming increasingly blurred due to Germany's inability to replace men and materiel at an acceptable rate. As a stopgap method to address the manpower shortage AOK 9 employed *c.* 10,000 Russian volunteers, known as *hiwis*, serving in support roles. In spring 1943 Model's AOK 9 was reinforced for a dedicated offensive role with five corps, consisting of a total of 22 divisions (6 panzer, 1 panzergrenadier and 15 infantry). In contrast, Clößner's 2.Panzerarmee had been stripped down to three corps with a total of 16 divisions (1 panzer, 1 panzergrenadier, 13 infantry and 1 security) in order to build up Model's army. The German Army had begun to rob from Peter to pay Paul in 1942, and by mid-1943 this method was causing serious problems, since offensives could only be conducted by making other sectors of the front dangerously weak.

Infantry

Model intended to use only 8 of his 15 infantry divisions from AOK 9 in an assault role for *Zitadelle*, with the others relegated to strictly defensive tasks. By mid-1943 Germany had lost the ability to replenish the manpower losses in its infantry divisions on the Eastern Front, and many units reduced the number of infantry battalions in each regiment from three to two. Among the eight infantry divisions involved in the *Zitadelle* offensive, only 258.Infanterie-Division and 78.Sturm-

Division had more than six infantry battalions, whereas two-thirds of Manstein's infantry divisions had nine infantry battalions. The average infantry battalion combat strength in AOK 9 was 425 troops out of an authorized 860; most infantry companies at the start of *Zitadelle* averaged about 80 men each. Furthermore, many of the replacements who arrived just before the start of *Zitadelle* were inadequately trained, and German reports after the battle mentioned serious deficiencies among the new troops. Some of the replacements were not even German but *Volksdeutsche* (ethnic Germans living outside of Germany); two replacement soldiers from Slovenia sent to 6.Infanterie-Division promptly defected to the Soviets. Consequently, Model's infantry divisions were quite fragile.

The one major exception to the sorry state of AOK 9's depleted infantry units was 78.Sturm-Division, which had been selected in January 1943 to be rebuilt as a reinforced assault formation. In addition to its six organic infantry battalions, 78.Sturm-Division was reinforced with two full-strength Jäger batallions. Altogether the division had nearly 6,000 combat troops and was augmented with heavy fire-support assets, including 12cm mortars, Nebelwerfer multiple rocket launchers and Sturmgeschütz-Abteilung 189 with 31 StuG III assault guns. Furthermore, 78.Sturm-Division was provided with very strong anti-tank capabilities, since it was equipped with 71 7.5cm Pak 40 and 25 self-propelled Marder II anti-tank guns. In contrast, most of AOK 9's infantry divisions were still dependent upon the inadequate 3.7cm and 5cm Pak guns and were fortunate if they had anything between 8 and 12 heavy anti-tank guns.

The German infantry divisions used in *Zitadelle* were only capable of significant offensive action when supported by assault guns. Here, infantry and a StuG III advance cautiously into the outskirts of a village. (Nik Cornish at www.Stavka.org.uk)

Artillery

Generalmajor Max Lindig was in command of Höherer Artillerie-Kommandeur (HArko) 307. He was responsible for coordinating fire from the subordinate corps and divisions, which comprised a total of 853 artillery pieces and 165 Nebelwerfer rocket launchers. However, the majority of Lindig's artillery consisted of 10.5cm and 15cm howitzers, which had limited ability to damage the kind of entrenched positions that had been prepared by Rokossovsky's Central Front. Lindig only had a few batteries of 21cm Mörsers and a few long-range 15cm and 17cm K18 cannons for counter-battery missions. One new artillery asset that Model's army received was the schwere Granatwerfer-Bataillon 19 (mot.), which was equipped with thirty-six 12cm Granatwerfer 42 mortars and forty-eight of the new Raupenschlepper Ost (RSO) caterpillar tractors. This was a handy infantry-support unit with excellent mobility, but typically for the lacklustre logistical build-up for *Zitadelle*, it had only been provided with 81 rounds per tube. Overall, the divisions in AOK 9 were provided with less new equipment than Manstein's forces, with Model's divisions averaging 35 artillery pieces compared to 48 for Manstein's divisions. Although 2.Panzer-Division and 4.Panzer-Division had received 24 Wespe and 18 Hummel self-propelled guns, the majority of Lindig's artillery still relied on horses and trucks as prime movers.

The German Army had been trying to mate the 15cm SIG 33 infantry howitzer to a tank hull since 1940 in order to provide heavy direct-fire support to assault troops. AOK 9 received Major Bruno Kahl's Sturmpanzer-Abteilung 216, which was equipped with 45 of the new Sturmpanzer IVs, as well as 10 of the earlier Sturmpanzer IIIs. The newer Sturmpanzers had better armour protection and their howitzer was well-suited to reducing Soviet strongpoints.

The only long-range weapons in AOK 9's artillery park were three 17cm Kanone 18 belonging to 1./schwere Artillerie-Abteilung 817, supporting XXIII Armeekorps. The 17cm Kanone could hurl a 68kg high-explosive shell out to 28km, giving it the ability to out-range all Soviet artillery. (Author's collection)

The 10.5cm le. FH18 howitzer was the standard German medium division-level artillery piece used throughout the war on the Eastern Front from 1941 to 1945. Although a reliable weapon, its high-explosive rounds were better suited to engaging targets in the open than the kind of fieldworks that Rokossovsky's troops had time to construct. Consequently, the German artillery preparations were not particularly effective in suppressing Soviet positions. (Bundesarchiv, Bild 101I-219-0561A-05)

Pioneers (pionieren)

Model realized that Soviet mines were going to be a major hindrance to the mobility of his forces during the initial phase of *Zitadelle* and he requested additional pioneer assets to clear these. However, unlike the British Army, which had made a serious effort to develop flail tanks and other rapid clearing technology in North Africa, the German Army had not expended much effort in improving its mine-clearing capabilities. Model's AOK 9 was provided with three Funklenk (Fkl – radio-controlled) companies of Borgward IV (BIV) demolition vehicles and two companies of panzer pioneers (panzer-pionieren) equipped with the smaller Goliath. Model attached the Funklenk companies to create breaches for the Ferdinands and Tigers, while the Goliaths were assigned to support 78.Sturm-Division. These pioneer units were tasked with creating lanes through the Soviet minefields for the German heavy armour by driving the demolition vehicles into the minefield and then detonating them to destroy nearby mines; the Germans estimated that four BIVs would be sufficient to create one lane. However, the pioneers had no expedient means to mark the lanes, which would be quite narrow and hard to follow. The mine-clearing for all the other units would have to be done by hand, by division and corps-level pioneer battalions. It was expected that it would take about two hours for a Pionier-Abteilung to create a breach through a 100m-deep minefield. Complicating the situation, the soil around Kursk was heavily magnetic and prevented the standard German electronic mine-detectors such as the Tempelhof 41 and Frankfort 40 from functioning properly. Consequently, most of Model's panzers would be restricted to advancing at a snail's pace, behind pioneers laboriously clearing minefields under-fire by hand.

German pioneers crawl along a gully during a breaching drill prior to *Zitadelle*. The *obergefreiter* in the front is carrying stakes to mark the cleared lanes. During the actual offensive, the engineers would have darkened their faces and worn camouflage on their helmets. Note the soldier with grenade at the ready – in case of unexpected close contact. (Author's collection)

Armour

Many histories give the impression that the Germans rebuilt and replenished all their panzer divisions during the lull period between April and June 1943. However, Model's armoured units only received a token infusion of new tanks. To make matters worse, the panzer divisions were no longer fully motorized due to heavy losses of wheeled vehicles in 1941 and 1942, and units like 18.Panzer-Division began *Zitadelle* with 1,868 horses on its roll. Heeresgruppe Mitte initially provided Model's AOK 9 with six panzer divisions for *Zitadelle*, and eventually gave him two more during the fight for the Orel salient, but each only had a single panzer battalion. Only two units – 2.Panzer-Division and 4.Panzer-Division, which were both allocated to Lemelsen's XXXXVII Panzerkorps – were brought back close to authorized strength. Overall, Model never had more than 800 tanks and assault guns at any one time during the campaign, and consequently his resources were somewhat lacking for such a large-scale mission.

In spring 1943 Germany decided to concentrate on upgrading the PzKpfw IV to serve as its main battle tank, until sufficient numbers of the new Panther were available. In March both new and existing PzKpfw IVs were fitted with *Schürzen* (side skirts) to improve protection against Soviet anti-tank rifles and 76.2mm high-explosive (HE) rounds. In April the PzKpfw IV Ausf. H model with the longer KwK 40 L/48 cannon and enhanced armoured protection entered production. This tank had an edge over the T-34/76 in terms of firepower, but its level of armoured protection was roughly similar and its mobility was inferior due to continued reliance on an underpowered petrol engine and a weak transmission. Model's command did receive some of the latest PzKpfw IV Ausf. H models. He also hoped to receive some of the new Pz V Panther tanks for *Zitadelle*, but all 200 of the new Panthers went to Manstein's Heeresgruppe Süd.

For *Zitadelle*, Model's main armoured strength thus consisted of 274 PzKpfw IV long-barrelled medium tanks in six panzer battalions. Yet one-third of his armour consisted of 202 obsolescent PzKpfw III tanks; only 89 of these were equipped with the long-barrelled 5cm gun, the rest featured either the short 5cm gun or 7.5cm howitzer. To compensate for the insufficient number of tanks available, Model's AOK 9 included seven Sturmgeschütz battalions in its order of battle, with a total of 196 StuG III and 31 StuH 42 assault guns. The StuG III Ausf. G with the long 7.7cm StuK 40 L/48 gun had an excellent anti-armour capability, while the StuH 42's 10.5cm howitzer was well suited to attacking

The Sturmpanzer mounted a 15cm howitzer atop a PzKpfw IV chassis in order to combine a powerful infantry support weapon with tactical mobility. The Sturmpanzer was excellent at reducing Soviet strongpoints and anti-tank positions, which caused the Soviets to single it out as a priority target to engage. (Ian Barter)

Although often praised for the superior firepower of its 8.8cm gun, during *Zitadelle* and the battle for the Orel salient the Tiger proved itself to be a giant with feet of clay. While it was true that the Tiger's thick armour made it almost invulnerable to the Soviet T-34's 76.2mm main gun at normal battlefield ranges, it failed to protect it from anti-tank mines, which quickly whittled down the number of operational tanks to a handful in just four days of combat. Furthermore, the Tiger's problematic transmission greatly undermined the vehicle's operational reliability and tactical mobility. (Ian Barter)

bunkers and towns. Nevertheless, Model's armoured forces were significantly inferior compared to the assets provided to Manstein's command, which fielded nine mechanized divisions for *Zitadelle*, with a total of 12 panzer battalions and over 1,400 tanks and assault guns.

Model did receive a single battalion of Pz VI Tiger tanks – Major Bernhard Sauvant's schwere Panzer-Abteilung 505 with 31 Tigers – but it began *Zitadelle* with only two of its three companies, and did not receive its third company until 8 July. The 56-ton Tiger was built around its lethal 8.8cm KwK 36 L/56 cannon and high-quality optical sights, which gave it the ability to destroy T-34s at ranges up to 1,500m and beyond. However, the Tiger I had limited tactical and negligible operational mobility, which greatly reduced its value in manoeuvre warfare. Furthermore, the Soviets were aware of the Tiger's capabilities after one had been captured near Leningrad in January 1943, and were hoping to use a combination of 85mm anti-aircraft guns and the SU-152 self-propelled gun to neutralize this threat.

In compensation for not receiving any Panthers, Model was provided with the new Ferdinand tank destroyers of Oberstleutnant Baron Ernst von Jungenfeld's schwere Panzerjäger Regiment 656. The Ferdinand was a spin-off from Porsche's failed entry into the heavy tank

The Ferdinand tank destroyer was initially misused as a breakthrough weapon in the first days of *Zitadelle* and suffered heavy losses due to mines. However, when used properly in defensive roles around Orel, the Ferdinand proved to be an outstanding anti-tank weapon. (Author's collection)

design competition, which was won by Henschel's Tiger. The 65-ton Ferdinands were cobbled together from Porsche's leftover hulls and the new long 8.8cm Pak 43/2 L/71 cannon in March and April 1943. Unlike the Tiger, the Ferdinand had not been used in combat prior to *Zitadelle* and the Red Army was unaware of its existence. The Ferdinand was heavier than the Tiger and even less mobile, but packed much heavier firepower. Moreover, its level of armoured protection made it almost invulnerable to 76.2mm gunfire. It was designed as a long-range tank destroyer, not a tank, so it lacked the coaxial machine gun that tanks normally employed for dealing with enemy infantry. While various sources have claimed that the Ferdinand was vulnerable to infantry at close range, there were actually only a handful of occasions during *Zitadelle* when Soviet infantry engaged isolated Ferdinands at close quarters. The two battalions of Ferdinands arrived near Orel on 12 June; each battalion consisted of three companies, each with 14 Ferdinands, plus 3 headquarters vehicles, giving a total of 45 Ferdinands per battalion. Model massed all his heavy armoured fighting vehicles in Harpe's XXXXI Panzerkorps and three panzer divisions in Lemelsen's XXXXVII Panzerkorps, but left a strong, uncommitted reserve known as Gruppe Esebeck, with two panzer divisions and 10.Panzergrenadier-Division.

Air support

Generaloberst Robert Ritter von Greim's Luftflotte 6 was tasked with supporting AOK 9's role in the *Zitadelle* offensive, using its 686 combat aircraft. The Luftwaffe had a significant edge in the offensive counter-air mission, with the technically advanced Fw-190A fighters and a substantial percentage of veteran pilots. One oddity was the presence of 15./Jagdgeschwader 51 (or Escuadrilla Azul No. 4 – 'Blue Squadron'), a Spanish volunteer unit equipped with Fw-190A fighters. General der Flieger Paul Deichmann's 1.Flieger-Division was also provided with four Stuka groups and seven bomber groups for *Zitadelle*. The Luftwaffe's plan for the northern sector was to rapidly gain air superiority over the battlefield and to direct all efforts towards providing effective close air support for Model's armour–infantry *schwerpunkt*.

Luftflotte 6 had four Jagdgruppen with 186 Fw-190A fighters to support AOK 9 during Operation *Zitadelle*. The Fw-190A-4 was faster and better armed than its primary opponents, the La-5 and Yak-7, and most German pilots were far more experienced. Consequently, Luftflotte 6 enjoyed a 4:1 or higher kill ratio on most days of *Zitadelle*. However, once Operation *Kutusov* began, Luftflotte 6's fighters had to fight three Soviet air armies. During July it lost a total of 133 Fw-190 fighters to all causes. (Author's collection)

Combat logistics

Despite the relative lull between April and June 1943, AOK 9's quartermasters were unable to meet the logistical requirements specified for Operation *Zitadelle* in Operations Orders No. 5 and No. 6. A combination of Soviet air raids, Soviet partisan activity and the daily requirements of even ordinary combat activity frustrated the German intent to build up a logistical surplus for *Zitadelle*. Indeed, not only did AOK 9's supply dumps have only 20 per-cent of the required fuel and 40 per-cent of the required ammunition by 4 July, but they actually held smaller quantities of each than they had held on 12 April. Like much of the Wehrmacht, AOK 9 was living a hand-to-mouth existence and was using more resources even on defence than Germany could provide. Most divisions started *Zitadelle* with two or three basic loads of ammunition and five *Verbrauchssatz* (the load of fuel required to move all vehicles in a unit 100km), of which 25 per-cent would be consumed on the first day of the offensive. The situation with personnel replacements was no better, with only 7,000 inadequately trained troops on hand in the Feld-Ersatz batallions to replace combat losses. Luftflotte 6's fuel situation was particularly difficult since there was no lull in air operations and the consumption of aviation fuel exceeded deliveries by a wide margin. Instead of possessing the logistical resources to sustain an 18-day operation as envisioned by the *Zitadelle* planners, AOK 9 and Luftflotte 6 only had the resources to conduct high-intensity offensive operations for about seven days. This inherent German logistical weakness is often ignored, but it played a major role in constricting AOK 9's role in *Zitadelle* as well as the subsequent defence of the Orel salient.

SOVIET

Rokossovsky's Central Front had been massively reinforced in order to conduct a deliberate defence of the northern shoulder of the Kursk salient. Unlike Model's AOK 9, Rokossovsky had plenty of infantry, and the quality of the Red Army's rifle units – particularly in the defence – had improved greatly since 1941–42. The days of German panzer units blasting through poorly equipped Soviet rifle divisions were over.

Infantry

Between 1941 and 1942, the Soviet infantry had been handicapped by a severe lack of trained junior officers. However, the Red Army was able to rectify this problem through a prodigious training effort. By 1943 Soviet infantry companies, battalions and regiments had gained a cadre

A Soviet rifle unit in fighting positions, overlooking flat terrain. Pukhov placed expendable penal companies in the forward security zone and units with large numbers of Caucasian troops in the first line of defence; his second and third lines, however, were manned with veteran Guards and Airborne divisions. Rokossovsky was willing to lose some ground in return for keeping his best units intact for the counter-offensive. (From the fonds of the RGAKFD in Krasnogorsk via Stavka)

of veteran officers who knew their business; no longer were they rank amateurs. Simple mistakes, like failing to cover obstacles with fire or tying in with flank units, were less likely to occur now. The Soviet rifle divisions in Central Front had been brought close to their authorized strength of 9,300 troops, and Rokossovsky deliberately put steady Guards and Airborne Rifle divisions in the areas where he expected the Germans to attack. This time, the panzers would find no untrained recruits to overrun, as they had done in the past.

The Soviets built their defence at Kursk around the rifle battalion strongpoint, which typically occupied an area of 2 square kilometres. Rifle regiments put two battalions up front, with the third 2km to the rear. The troops and weapons were protected from German bombardments by trenches and dugouts. Each strongpoint was tied in with anti-tank batteries and minefields to protect them from armoured attacks. These strongpoints were very tough to crack, particularly when manned by steady troops, and the Germans would have to defeat each in turn. The old Blitzkrieg style of warfare – which Hitler hoped to pull off once again at Kursk – simply could not work against this style of defence.

Artillery

Rokossovsky enjoyed an immense superiority in artillery over Model's AOK 9, and Soviet artillery organization and tactics were maturing rapidly by mid-1943. In March of that year, the Red Army began forming artillery corps, which provided an unprecedented level of fire support. General-Major Nikolai V. Ignatov's 4th Artillery Corps was assigned to provide direct support to Pukhov's 13th Army, with its 5th and 12th Artillery divisions and 5th Guards Mortar Division. Ignatov's corps comprised over 30,000 troops with 496 artillery pieces, 216 heavy mortars and 192 multiple rocket launchers. Even greater artillery support was set aside for Operation *Kutusov*, with Bryansk Front receiving 2nd, 7th and 8th Artillery corps to support its attacks. For the first time in the war, the Soviets were able to mass hundreds of tube and rocket artillery systems to support operations on a single axis, which completely outclassed their German artillery counterparts. In a novel tactic, the Soviet artillerymen also intended to use multiple rocket launcher barrages to disrupt German armoured concentrations, particularly at breach sites.

Rokossovsky knew that Model's armour would eventually penetrate at least some parts of the obstacle belts, and he relied upon massed anti-tank artillery fire to halt any breakthroughs. Each rifle battalion strongpoint had four

A battery of ML-20 152mm howitzers moving into position in preparation for the German offensive. Rokossovsky enjoyed a large superiority in heavy artillery, and he intended to use it to break up large German assault concentrations. 4th Artillery Corps proved to be a Soviet trump card that the Germans could not overcome. (From the fonds of the RGAKFD in Krasnogorsk via Stavka)

45mm anti-tank guns, which were a threat to German medium tanks at close range. Altogether, Pukhov's 13th Army had 44 anti-tank strongpoints in its first line of defence, with about 50 76.2mm ZIS-3 and 150 45mm anti-tank guns. The second line of defence had 34 anti-tank strongpoints with 160 anti-tank guns, and the third line of defence had 60 anti-tank strongpoints with 342 anti-tank guns. Rokossovsky's mobile anti-tank reserve consisted of three anti-tank brigades, each with 40 76.2mm ZIS-3 and 20 45mm or 57mm anti-tank guns. The Red Army reckoned that an anti-tank brigade, with proper infantry support, could stop a German panzer division.

Armour

Rokossovsky had 1,749 tanks in Central Front to oppose Model's 800 tanks and assault guns. His main armoured reserve was in Rodin's 2nd Tank Army, which had a total of 456 tanks, but he also had the 9th and 19th Tank corps as independent reserves. In addition, 13th Army had been augmented with one tank brigade and five tank regiments for infantry support. About 70 percent of the Soviet armour consisted of the T-34/76 Model 1942 or Model 1943, with the rest consisting of 436 T-60 and T-70 light tanks, about 40 KV-1 heavy tanks and few dozen British-built Valentines and Churchills. Despite all the rhetoric about Soviet tank production surpassing German tank production, the Red Army still did not have sufficient T-34 medium tanks to completely equip its tank brigades. It was forced to continue using the T-70 light tank in all its tank brigades at Kursk, even though this vehicle was no match even for the obsolescent German PzKpfw III.

The Soviet T-34 medium tank had been vastly superior to all German tanks at the beginning of the war. However, it had gradually lost its technical superiority as the enemy introduced better tanks. Moreover, Stavka resisted improvements that would reduce current monthly production of the T-34. Outfitted with a new hexagonal turret, the T-34/76 Model 1943 was a slight improvement over previous models, but its 76.2mm F-34 cannon could not defeat either the Tiger or Ferdinand at typical battlefield ranges of 500 to 800m. Indeed, even the upgraded PzKpfw IV Ausf. H could defeat the T-34/76 at ranges beyond the Soviet tank's ability to effectively hit back. While the T-34 was still a formidable defensive tank, particularly when deployed in hull-down positions, it no longer had the shock effect that it had enjoyed between 1941 and 1942. Soviet industry was working on efforts to upgrade the T-34 or mount larger guns on assault gun tanks, but neither solution would be ready in time for the battle of Kursk.

Soviet reinforcements arrived in great numbers to bolster Rokossovsky's defence in the northern sector of the Kursk salient, including many T-34 tanks with the new hexagonal turret and well-equipped infantry units. Not only was the Red Army of mid-1943 better equipped, but its soldiers were also more confident of victory after Stalingrad. The conflict was increasingly becoming a war of liberation, and every advance to the west increased Soviet morale at the expense of that of the Germans. (Author's collection)

Soviet Il-2 Sturmovik ground attack aircraft. The 16th Air Army started *Zitadelle* with about 240 Il-2s, and lost 90 in six days of combat. The Il-2 proved very vulnerable to the 2cm cannons on the Fw-190A-4 fighter, and Soviet fighter cover was often inadequate in the first days of the German offensive. Nevertheless, the Il-2s played a greater role once German fighter strength began to ebb during the evacuation of the Orel salient. (Courtesy of the Central Museum of the Armed Forces, Moscow via Stavka)

Rokossovsky was provided with two regiments of the new SU-152 self-propelled gun, which could theoretically destroy or disable a Tiger with its heavy 152mm rounds (it was as yet untested in the tank destroyer role). Soviet accounts have tended to exaggerate the combat debut of the SU-152 at Kursk, lauding it as the infamous *Zvierboy* or 'animal hunter', but very few saw action during *Zitadelle*. In the interim, each tank corps was provided with a battalion of 12 towed 85mm M1939 anti-aircraft guns to be used as expedient anti-tank guns. Although these weapons could penetrate the frontal armour of a Tiger tank at 1,000m and side armour at 1,500m, they were large, bulky guns that were difficult to camouflage and deploy in the forward battle area.

Air support

General-Leytenant Sergei I. Rudenko's 16th Air Army (Vozdushnaya Armiya – VA) provided air support to Rokossovsky's Central Front with about 950 operational combat aircraft at the start of *Zitadelle*. The VVS aviation regiments were now well equipped with up-to-date fighters like the Yak-7 and La-5, as well as an increasing number of veteran pilots. While both the Yak-7 and La-5 were technically inferior in speed and firepower to the German Fw-190A fighter, their overall 2:1 numerical advantage helped to level the playing field. One oddity in the VVS line up was the Normandie-Niemen Eskadrilya (Groupe de Chasse GC 3 Normandie), a Free-French unit that became operational in the USSR in March 1943. The French squadron was equipped with Yak-1 fighters and flew with 1st Air Army in support of Western Front during Operation *Kutusov*. Rudenko also had large numbers of sturdy Il-2 Sturmovik and Pe-2 bombers to provide close air support to Rokossovsky's ground troops. However, due to the 2cm cannons on the Fw 190 fighter, the Il-2 Sturmovik was no longer as resistant to fighter attack as it had been in 1941 and 1942 and found it more difficult to survive in contested air space. Rudenko's 16th Air Army was provided with Yak-9T fighter-bombers, armed with two 37mm guns in underwing pods and PTAB anti-tank bombs.

Mine warfare

Although the Red Army had employed land mines in defensive combat during 1941 and 1942, their effect had been purely tactical and provided no great impediment to German armoured operations. However, at Kursk the Soviets had the luxury of several months to emplace a total of 943,000 mines around the salient, which posed a serious obstacle for the two German armoured pincers. In Rokossovsky's sector, 13th Army laid 50,000 anti-tank and 35,000 anti-personnel mines across its 32km-wide front, which gave a density of over 2,600 mines per kilometre of front. By July 1943 there were no gaps or places to bypass the minefields, unlike in the past. The new Red Army mine warfare doctrine issued in April 1943 stressed depth in minefields, which meant that Model's troops would have to fight their way through several layers of minefields, each up to 100m in depth. About 80 per-cent of the mines were emplaced in the first line of defence, with far fewer committed to the second and third lines. The Soviet TM-38 and TM-41 anti-tank mines were powerful enough to damage the track on any German armoured vehicle, but were unlikely to do more than this. Damaged track blocks or roadwheels could be replaced in less than an hour, when not under fire; however, if the roadwheel arm assembly had been warped or sheared off by the explosion, this could not be quickly repaired. Soviet sappers mixed in wooden PMD-6 anti-personnel mines with the anti-tank mines, which were difficult to detect with electronic minesweepers and posed a significant hazard for German infantry.

The new Soviet mine warfare doctrine also emphasized the importance of motorized 'mobile obstacle detachments' (*podvishnyi otriad zagrazhdenii* or POZ), whose role was to lay mines in front of advancing enemy units. Pukhov's 13th Army had five POZ, each of platoon or company size; they were mounted in trucks and capable of creating new minefields in a matter of hours. If the Germans had been aware how dangerous these units were, they would have prioritized their detection and destruction by the Luftwaffe. In any case, mine warfare was of decisive importance for the Soviet strategy of immobilizing and destroying Model's panzer units.

Soviet sappers laying mines in the forward security area, while under fire. The Germans had never encountered mine warfare on this scale before and had limited ability to breach dense minefields that were covered by direct fire. More than any other branch, the Soviet sappers shaped the battle of Kursk and determined its outcome. (Author's collection)

ORDER OF BATTLE

GERMAN FORCES IN THE OREL SALIENT, 5 JULY 1943

AOK 9 (GENERALOBERST WALTHER MODEL)

XX Armeekorps (General der Artillerie Rudolf Freiherr von Roman)

45.Infanterie-Division

72.Infanterie-Division

137.Infanterie-Division

251.Infanterie-Division

XXXXVI Panzerkorps (General der Infanterie Hans Zorn)

7.Infanterie-Division (Generalleutnant Fritz-Georg von Rappard)

    2./Sturmgeschütz-Abteilung 909

31.Infanterie-Division (Generalleutnant Friedrich Hoßbach)

    1. and 3./Sturmgeschütz-Abteilung 909

    schwere Granatwerfer-Bataillon (mot.) 18 [12cm]

    leichte Artillerie-Abteilung 430 [10.5cm howitzer]

    3./schwere Artillerie-Abteilung 637 [21cm Mörser]

102.Infanterie-Division

258.Infanterie-Division (Generalleutnant Hanskurt Höcker)

    StossGruppe von Manteuffel (Jägerbataillon 9, 10, 11)

    6./Panzer-Regiment 29 [PzKpfw IV]

    2./Panzerjäger-Abteilung 2 [Marder]

Arko 101

    schwere Artillerie-Abteilung 611 [10cm]

    3./schwere Artillerie-Abteilung 620 [15cm cannon]

    II./Artillerie-Regiment 47 [10cm cannon/15cm howitzer]

    IV./Artillerie-Regiment 104 [15cm howitzers]

XXXXI Panzerkorps

(General der Panzertruppen Josef Harpe)

18.Panzer-Division (Generalmajor Karl-Wilhelm von Schlieben)

86.Infanterie-Division (Generalleutnant Helmuth Weidling)

schwere Panzerjäger-Abteilung 654 [Ferdinand]

    Panzerkompanie (Fkl) 313

    Sturmgeschütz-Abteilung 177

292.Infanterie-Division (Generalleutnant Wolfgang von Kluge, WIA 20 July)

schwere Panzerjäger-Abteilung *653* [Ferdinand]

    Panzerkompanie (Fkl) 314

    Sturmgeschütz-Abteilung 244

schwere Panzerjäger Regiment *656*

    Sturmpanzer-Abteilung 216 [45 Sturmpanzer]

XXXXVII Panzerkorps

(General der Panzertruppen Joachim Lemelsen)

2.Panzer-Division (Generalleutnant Vollrath Lübbe)

9.Panzer-Division (Generalleutnant Walter Scheller)

20.Panzer-Division (Generalmajor Mortimer von Kessel)

6.Infanterie-Division (Generalleutnant Horst Großmann)

1. and 2./schwere Panzer-Abteilung 505 [31 Tiger]

Panzerkompanie (Fkl) 312 (Leutnant Nolte)

Sturmgeschütz-Abteilung 245 [36 assault guns]

Sturmgeschütz-Abteilung 904 [36 assault guns]

XXIII Armeekorps

(General der Infanterie Johannes Frießner)

216.Infanterie-Division (Generalmajor Friedrich-August Schack)

    Grenadier-Regiment 533 [from 383.Infanterie-Division]

    Sturmgeschütz-Abteilung 185

78.Sturm-Division (Generalleutnant Hans Traut)

    Panzer-Pionier-Kompanie 811 and 813

    Sturmgeschütz-Abteilung 189

    schwere Granatwerfer-Bataillon (mot.) 5 [12cm mortars/RSO]

    leichte Artillerie-Abteilung 426 [10.5cm howitzers/RSO]

    1. and 2./schwere Artillerie-Abteilung 635 [21cm Mörser]

    schwere Artillerie-Abteilung 422 [10cm cannon/15cm howitzers]

    Jäger-Bataillon 8

383.Infanterie-Division (Oberst Edmund Hoffmeister)

    Grenadier-Regiment 87 [from 36.Infanterie-Division (mot.)]

Arko 112

    1./schwere Artillerie-Abteilung 817 [17cm cannon]

    4./leichte Artillerie-Abteilung 69 [10.5cm]

    leichte Artillerie-Abteilung 709

    leichte Artillerie-Abteilung 59

    leichte Artillerie-Abteilung 851 [captured 122mm guns]

    schwere Artillerie-Abteilung 859 [21cm Mörser]

    schwere Artillerie-Abteilung 848 [15cm howitzers]

    II./schwere Artillerie-Abteilung 66 [15cm howitzers]

    I., II. and III./Werfer-Regiment 51 [15cm and 21cm]

Gruppe Esebeck (AOK 9 Reserve)

4.Panzer-Division (Generalleutnant Dietrich von Saucken)

12.Panzer-Division (Generalmajor Erpo Freiherr von Bodenhausen)

10. Panzergrenadier-Division (Generalleutnant August Schmidt)

2.PANZERARMEE (GENERAL DER INFANTERIE ERICH-HEINRICH CLÖSSNER)

XXXV Armeekorps (General der Infanterie Lothar Rendulic)

34.Infanterie-Division

56.Infanterie-Division

262.Infanterie-Division

299.Infanterie-Division

36.Infanterie-Division (mot.)

LIII Armeekorps (General der Infanterie Friedrich Gollwitzer)

25.Panzergrenadier-Division

208.Infanterie-Division

211.Infanterie-Division

293.Infanterie-Division

211.Sicherungs-Division (less elements)

LV Armeekorps (General der Infanterie Erich Jaschke)

110.Infanterie-Division

134.Infanterie-Division

296.Infanterie-Division

339.Infanterie-Division

5.Panzer-Division

Army Reserve

112.Infanterie-Division

707.Infanterie-Division

REINFORCEMENTS

12 July

8.Panzer-Division from Vitebsk (3.Panzerarmee)

18–20 July

Panzergrenadier-Division Großdeutschland from Heeresgruppe Süd

26.Infanterie-Division from AOK 2

253.Infanterie-Division from AOK 4

AOK 9 tank strength, 5 July 1943

Unit	Heavy		Medium		Light			Total
	Tiger	Ferdinand	PzKpfw III	PzKpfw IV	Pz II	PzBef		
2.Panzer-Division			40	60	12	6		118
4.Panzer-Division			15	80	6	0		101
9.Panzer-Division			38	30	1	6		75
12.Panzer-Division			36	37	6	4		83
18.Panzer-Division			30	34	5	3		72
20.Panzer-Division			17	49	9	7		82
schwere Panzerjäger-Regiment 656	0	90						90
schwere Panzer-Abteilung 505	31	0	19	0				50
TOTAL	31	90	195	290	39	26		671

LUFTWAFFE

Luftflotte 6 (Generaloberst Robert Ritter von Greim), HQ in Orel

1.Flieger-Division (General der Flieger Paul Deichmann)

III./Kampfgeschwader 1 (Ju-88)

Stab, II. and III./Kampfgeschwader 4 (He-111)

Stab, II and III./Kampfgeschwader 51 (Ju-88)

Stab, I. and III./Kampfgeschwader 53 (He-111)

Stab, I., II. and III./Sturzkampfgeschwader 1 (Ju-87)

III./Sturzkampfgeschwader 3 (Ju-87)

I./Zerstörergeschwader 1 (Bf-110)

Stab, I., III., IV. and 15.(Span)/Jagdgeschwader 51 (Fw-190A)

I./Jagdgeschwader 54 (Fw-190)

Stab. 1., 2. and 3./Nahaufklärungsgruppe 4 (Bf-109)

Luftwaffe operational strength at Kursk

Type	Model	Number available
Day fighter	Fw-190	186
Night fighter	Bf-109	39
Level bombers	Ju-88	92
	He-111	152
Ground attack	Ju-87	159
	Bf-110	58
TOTAL		686

12.Flak-Division (Generalleutnant Ernst Buffa)

10. Flak-Brigade (Generalmajor Karl Schuchardt)

SOVIET FORCES AROUND THE OREL SALIENT, 5 JULY 1943

CENTRAL FRONT
(GENERAL KONSTANTIN K. ROKOSSOVSKY)

13th Army (General-Leytenant Nikolai P. Pukhov)

17th Guards Rifle Corps (General-Leytenant Andrei L. Bondarev): 6th, 70th and 75th Guards Rifle divisions

18th Guards Rifle Corps (General-Major Ivan M. Afonin): 2nd, 3rd and 4th Airborne Guards Rifle divisions

15th Rifle Corps (General-Major Ivan I. Liudnikov): 8th, 74th and 148th Rifle divisions

29th Rifle Corps (General-Major Afanasy N. Slyshkin): 15th, 81st and 307th Rifle divisions

4th Artillery Corps (General-Major Nikolai V. Ignatov): 5th, 12th Artillery divisions, 5th Guards Mortar Division

129th Tank Brigade

27th and 30th Guards Separate Tank regiments

43rd, 58th and 237th Separate Tank regiments

48th Army (General-Leytenant Prokofy Romanenko)

42nd Rifle Corps (General-Major Konstantin S. Kolganov): 16th, 202nd and 399th Rifle divisions

73rd, 137th, 143rd and 170th Rifle divisions

45th, 193rd, 299th Separate Tank regiments

65th Army (General-Leytenant Pavel I. Batov)

18th Rifle Corps (General-Major Ivan I. Ivanov): 69th, 149th and 246th Rifle divisions

27th Rifle Corps (General-Major Filipp M. Cherokmanov): 60th and 193rd Rifle divisions

37th Guards Rifle Division, 181st, 194th and 354th Rifle divisions

29th Guards Separate Tank Regiment

40th, 84th and 255th Separate Tank regiments

70th Army (General-Leytenant Ivan V. Galanin)

28th Rifle Corps (General-Major Aleksandr N. Nechaev): 132nd, 211th and 280th Rifle divisions

102nd, 106th, 140th and 162nd Rifle divisions

1st Guards Artillery Division

240th, 251st and 259th Separate Tank regiments

2nd Tank Army (General-Leytenant Aleksei G. Rodin;

General-Leytenant Semen I. Bogdanov from 2 August 1941)

3rd Tank Corps (General-Major Maksim D. Sinenko)

16th Tank Corps (General-Major Vasily E. Grigor'ev)

11th Guards Tank Brigade (Polkovnik Nikolai Bubnov)

Under front control

9th Tank Corps (General-Leytenant Semen I. Bogdanov)

19th Tank Corps (General-Major Ivan D. Vasil'ev)

16th Air Army (General-Leytenant Sergei I. Rudenko)

6th Fighter Aviation Corps (Isrebitelnyi Aviatsionnyi Korpus – IAK): 273rd Fighter Aviation Division, 279th Fighter Aviation Division: 157th, 163rd and 347th Fighter regiments (Yak-1/7/9), 92nd and 486th Fighter regiments (La-5)

1st Guards Fighter Aviation Division (GIAD): 30th and 67th Guards Fighter regiments (P-39), 53rd, 54th and 55th Guards Fighter regiments (Yak-1)

3rd Bomber Aviation Corps (BAK): 241st and 301st Bomber divisions: 24th, 34th, 54th, 128th and 779th Bomber regiments (Pe-2) and 96th Guards Bomber Regiment (Pe-2)

6th Composite Air Corps (SAK): 221st Bomber Division: 57th, 745th Bomber regiments and 8th Guards Bomber Regiment (A-20); 282nd Fighter Division: 127th, 517th and 774th Fighter regiments (Yak-1)

283rd Fighter Division: 56th Guards, 176th and 563rd Fighter regiments (Yak-1), 519th Fighter Regiment (Yak-7)

286th Fighter Division: 165th, 721st, 739th Fighter regiments (La-5) and 896th Fighter Regiment (Yak-1)

299th Ground Attack Aviation Division (ShAD): 41st, 217th, 218th, 431st and 874th Ground Attack Aviation regiments (Il-2)

2nd Guards Ground Attack Aviation Division (GShAD): 58th, 59th, 78th and 79th Guards Ground Attack Aviation regiments (Il-2)

Soviet operational aircraft strength

Type	Model	Number serviceable (estimated)
Fighters	Yak-1/7/9	300
	La-5	110
	P-39	40
Day bombers	Pe-2	175
	A-20	85
Ground attack	Il-2	241
TOTAL		951

WESTERN FRONT (GENERAL VASILY D. SOKOLOVSKY)

11th Guards Army

(General-Polkovnik Ivan Khristoforovich Bagramyan)

8th Guards Rifle Corps (General-Major Petr F. Malyshev): 11th, 26th and 83rd Guards Rifle divisions

16th Guards Rifle Corps (General-Major Afanasii V. Lapshov): 1st, 16th and 31st Guards Rifle divisions, 169th Rifle Division

36th Guards Rifle Corps (General-Major Aleksandr S. Ksenefontov): 5th, 18th and 84th Guards Rifle divisions

108th and 217th Rifle divisions

8th Artillery Corps (General-Leytenant Nikolai F. Salichko): 3rd and 6th Artillery divisions

14th Artillery Division

10th, 29th and 43rd Guards Tank brigades

213th Tank Brigade

2nd Guards Separate Heavy Tank Regiment

4th Guards Separate Tank Regiment

50th Army (General-Leytenant Ivan V. Boldin)

38th Rifle Corps (General-Major Aleksei D. Tereshkov): 17th, 326th and 413th Rifle divisions

49th, 64th, 212th and 324th Rifle divisions

196th Tank Brigade

Under front control

1st Tank Corps (General-Major Vasily V. Butkov)

5th Tank Corps (General-Major Mikhail G. Sakhno)

2nd Guards Tank Brigade

94th, 120th and 187th Tank brigades

56th Guards, 161st, 233rd and 248th Separate Tank regiments

371st Rifle Division

36th Rifle Brigade

1st Air Army (General-Leytenant Mikhail M. Gromov)

BRYANSK FRONT

(GENERAL-POLKOVNIK MARKIAN M. POPOV)

3rd Army (General-Leytenant Aleksandr V. Gorbatov)

41st Rifle Corps (General-Major Viktor K. Urbanovich): 235th, 308th and 380th Rifle divisions

269th, 283rd and 342nd Rifle divisions

82nd, 114th Separate Tank regiments

20th Artillery Division

61st Army (General-Leytenant Pavel Belov)

9th Guards Rifle Corps (General-Major Arkady A. Boreiko): 12th, 76th and 77th Guards Rifle divisions

97th, 110th, 336th, 356th and 415th Rifle divisions

68th Tank Brigade

36th Separate Tank Regiment

7th Artillery Corps (General-Major Pavel M. Korol'kov): 16th and 17th Artillery divisions, 2nd Guards Heavy Mortar Division

63rd Army

(General-Leytenant Vladimir Yakovlevich Kolpakchi)

5th, 41st, 129th, 250th, 287th, 348th and 397th Rifle divisions

2nd Artillery Corps (General-Leytenant Mikhail M. Barsukov): 13th and 15th Artillery divisions, 3rd Guards Heavy Mortar divisions

231st Separate Tank Regiment

Under front control

1st Guards Tank Corps (General-Major Mikhail F. Panov)

25th Rifle Corps (General-Major Petr V. Pererva): 186th, 283rd and 362nd Rifle divisions

11th, 12th, 13th, 26th Guards Separate Tank regiments

253rd Separate Tank Regiment

15th Air Army (General-Leytenant Nikolai F. Naumenko)

REINFORCEMENTS

12 July

11th Army (General-Leytenant Ivan I. Fedyuninsky)

53rd Rifle Corps (General-Major Ivan A. Gartsev): 135th, 197th and 369th Rifle divisions

4th, 96th, 260th, 273rd and 323rd Rifle divisions

225th Separate Tank Regiment

13–14 July

3rd Guards Tank Army (General-Leytenant Pavel S. Rybalko)

12th [6th Guards] Tank Corps (General-Major Mitrofan I. Zin'kovich)

15th [7th Guards] Tank Corps (General-Major Filipp N. Rudkin)

2nd [7th Guards] Mechanized Corps (General-Major Ivan M. Korchagin)

91st Separate Tank Brigade

20th Tank Corps (General-Leytenant Ivan G. Lazarev)

17 July

25th Tank Corps (General-Major Fedor G. Anikushkin)

18 July

4th Guards Tank Army (General-Leytenant Vasily M. Badanov)

11th Tank Corps (General-Major Nikolai N. Radkevich)

30th Tank Corps (Polkovnik Georgiy S. Rodin)

6th Guards Mechanized Corps (General-Major Aleksandr I. Akimov)

25 July

2nd Guards Cavalry Corps (General-Leytenant Vladimir V. Kriukov): 3rd, 4th Guards Cavalry divisions, 20th Cavalry Division

AOK 9'S OFFENSIVE, 5–11 JULY 1943

THE BUILD-UP

The three months prior to *Zitadelle* are often recorded as comprising a lull with little or no activity. While it is true that there were no major battles fought in this period, both sides aggressively used their airpower to try to limit each other's build-up for the main event. The VVS (Military Air Forces) mounted a series of large air raids against the rail stations in Bryansk and Orel in May and June to disrupt AOK 9's logistical preparations for *Zitadelle*. Operating both day and night, the Soviet bombers enjoyed considerable success and managed to destroy a number of trains and supplies. Luftflotte 6's fighters were using more fuel on counter-air operations in this period than they were receiving, which prevented the accumulation of a significant fuel stockpile for *Zitadelle*. The Luftwaffe also responded by conducting airstrikes against the Soviet rail stations in and around Kursk, but suffered heavy losses in May and June.

In addition to air combat, considerable rear-area partisan activity and artillery duels took place along the frontline. Even in the relatively 'quiet' month of June 1943, AOK 9 was firing more than 45 tonnes of artillery ammunition per day. Four of the eight infantry divisions assigned to attack in *Zitadelle* remained in the frontline, which constrained their ability to retrain for the offensive. In order to curb partisan activity prior to *Zitadelle*, AOK 9 mounted Operation *Zigeunerbaron* (Gypsy Baron), employing five divisions for three weeks. Model also required units to construct defences in depth throughout the Orel salient, which meant plenty of digging. In short, neither Luftflotte 6 nor AOK 9 received adequate time for training or rest prior to *Zitadelle*.

A Staffel of Ju-87 Stukas dives to attack targets. Luftflotte 6 started *Zitadelle* with four groups, equipped with a total of 159 Stukas. Although Stuka losses were relatively light during *Zitadelle*, Luftflotte 6 lost a total of 69 Stukas to all causes throughout July 1943. (Bundesarchiv, Bild 101I-646-5188-17)

5 JULY

Unlike Heeresgruppe Süd, Model did not intend to telegraph his punch by conducting a preliminary attack to eliminate Rokossovsky's forward outpost line. However, he did authorize his frontline divisions to begin quietly clearing lanes through the outer minefields on the night of 4/5 July. Rokossovsky knew that the German offensive was imminent and he directed his frontline units to gather additional information. Kapitan Nikolai S. Kolesov, commander of the scouts of the 15th Rifle Division 'Sivashkaya', established ambushes near Tagino; these secured a German prisoner after a skirmish with a sapper party from 6.Infanterie-Division. Once removed to Soviet lines and interrogated by intelligence chief Major Pavel S. Savinov, the prisoner confirmed that AOK 9 would attack within a matter of hours. Zhukov was present in Rokossovsky's headquarters when the intelligence arrived and the two senior officers agreed that some effort should be made to disrupt the impending German offensive.

Always eager to 'do something', Zhukov ordered Rokossovsky to immediately conduct a counter-barrage against the German forward positions in the 13th Army sector. At 0220 hours Pukhov's gunners began a ragged barrage that gradually gained in volume as more batteries were alerted and joined in. Yet it was impossible for Soviet forward observers to provide corrections in the darkness, and this was essentially an unplanned area suppression mission. In some sectors, such as that of 20.Panzer-Division, the Germans noted 'sporadic shelling' with only a limited number of rounds fired. In his memoirs, Zhukov blamed Rokossovsky for opening fire 'prematurely' and ignored his own role in this mistake. At best, Pukhov's counter-barrage caused minor disruption among the German assault elements, but it confirmed that the Soviets were alert and knew that *Zitadelle* was about to begin.

At 0425 hours, the aircraft of Deichmann's 1.Flieger-Division began flying across the German frontlines to attack Soviet forward positions and known artillery concentrations. Five minutes later Lindig (commander of HArko 307) began his own 80-minute artillery preparation against 13th Army's forward positions. The bulk of the German artillery, 10.5cm l.FH18 howitzers and Nebelwerfers, could only fire to a depth of 2–6km into the Soviet positions, which meant that they could not disrupt the Soviet 122mm and 152mm batteries that were located further to the rear. While the small number of German 10cm s.K18 and 15cm K18 cannons could strike targets to a depth of 12–16km, best results could only be achieved in daylight and with aerial forward observers. For the first hour of *Zitadelle*, Lindig's howitzers and Deichmann's Stukas churned up Pukhov's first line of defence with

A German 15cm Nebelwerfer 41 crew reloads rockets for another barrage. AOK 9 had a total of four Nebelwerfer battalions, each with eighteen 15cm rocket launchers, supporting XXIII Armeekorps and XXXXI Panzerkorps. Given that its range was barely 2km, the Nebelwerfer 41 had to be deployed just behind the front. (Bundesarchiv, Bild 101I-022-2943-20)

AOK 9's attack, 5 July 1943.

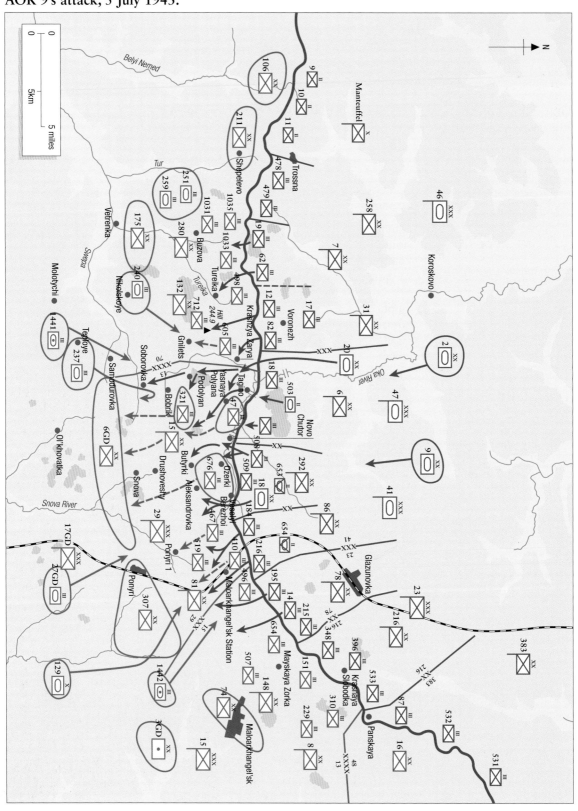

high explosives. Yet the German preparation struck the outer layer of Rokossovsky's defences and was only capable of suppressing strongpoints, not destroying them. In turn, Pukhov directed his corps artillery not to remain silent during the German barrage, but to return the fire.

Model decided to begin his offensive with eight infantry divisions and 20.Panzer-Division. However, AOK 9 did not begin its offensive in one simultaneous 'over-the-top' moment, but in staggered fashion. The first German attacks began in the east at 0530 hours, where General der Infanterie Johannes Frießner's XXIII Armeekorps committed 78.Sturm-Division and 216. and 383. Infantry divisions against the right flank of 13th Army; their main objective was to capture the town of Maloarkhangel'sk. This would secure the eastern flank of the German penetration and unhinge Pukhov's right flank. Pioneers from Generalleutnant Hans Traut's 78.Sturm-Division, using Goliath demolition vehicles, were able to breach the minefields covered by the Soviet 148th Rifle Division, and the assault troops from five battalions were then able to cross over 200m of open ground in order to attack strongpoints belonging to the 496th and 654th Rifle regiments. Due to the massed fires of Nebelwerfers, 12cm mortars and assault guns, Traut's 78.Sturm-Division was able to suppress some of the forward Soviet positions sufficiently for the infantry to overrun the first line of trenches. However, 78.Sturm-Division soon became bogged down in reducing the forward Soviet battalions and only succeeded in advancing c. 3,500–4,000m by evening. Frießner's other assault division (216.Infanterie-Division) attacked the frontline positions of 8th Rifle Division with six infantry battalions and the assault guns of Sturmgeschütz-Abteilung 185, but achieved only a limited advance of less than 2km. The 383.Infanterie-Division was supposed to launch a diversionary attack against the boundary of 13th Army and 48th Army near Panskaya, but its weak effort was easily repulsed. By day's end, Frießner's corps had accomplished very little and was still more than 6km from the edge of Maloarkhangel'sk. Traut's 78.Sturm-Division was in poor shape, but General-Major Ivan I. Liudnikov's 15th Rifle Corps still maintained an intact line of defence and quickly replaced its frontline losses with reserves.

The main German effort was aimed at the middle of Pukhov's front, in the sector held by General-Major Afanasy N. Slyshkin's 29th Rifle Corps. The latter consisted of Polkovnik Vladimir N. Dzhandzhgava's 15th Rifle Division 'Sivashkaya' and General-Major Aleksandr B. Barinov's 81st Rifle Division in the first echelon, and 307th Rifle Division in the second echelon. Both frontline divisions defended 9–10km-wide frontages, with two rifle regiments in their first line and one regiment in the second line. Pukhov initially kept his armour further back in 13th Army's second line of defence, so Slyshkin had only a handful of dug-in tanks to support his forward positions. Model's *schwerpunkt* focused Lemelsen's XXXXVII Panzerkorps and Harpe's XXXXI Panzerkorps on smashing through Slyshkin's defences, pitting three infantry and two panzer divisions against six rifle regiments.

A Soviet 57mm ZIS-2 anti-tank gun prepares to engage targets. The ZIS-2 had better armour penetration than the larger ZIS-3, but by 1943 it was normally used only by specialized corps-level anti-tank units. Although many accounts mention the ZIS-2's inability to defeat the Tiger heavy tank, it had no difficulty knocking out the far more numerous PzKpfw III and PzKpfw IV medium tanks. (From the fonds of the RGAKFD in Krasnogorsk via Stavka)

Soviet infantry awaiting a German attack. The soldier in the foreground has three RGD-33 anti-personnel grenades and two RPG-40 anti-tank grenades. Soviet infantry proved very tenacious on the defence during *Zitadelle*, and few positions were given up without a determined fight. Note the deep *balka* (ravine) in front of the Soviet position – a natural anti-tank ditch. (Courtesy of the Central Museum of the Armed Forces, Moscow via Stavka)

Lemelsen began his attack before 0600 hours. Generalleutnant Helmuth Weidling's 86.Infanterie-Division was tasked with attacking straight down the Kursk–Orel rail line. Weidling deployed his Grenadier-Regiment 216 on the east side of the rail line, supported by Ferdinands from schwere Panzerjäger-Abteilung 654 and assault guns from Sturmgeschütz-Abteilung 177, while Grenadier-Regiment 184 attacked on the west side of the rail line. Weidling was attacking on a narrow 4km-wide front with four infantry battalions, supported by a mass of armour, but this was also the avenue of approach that Rokossovsky expected the Germans to use. The 410th Rifle Regiment from Barinov's 81st Rifle Division held this sector, supported by a great deal of artillery. Panzerkompanie (Fkl) 313 was supposed to clear three lanes through the mines east of the rail line using Borgward IV demolition vehicles, but lost seven vehicles to accidents and artillery fire; only one narrow lane was cleared. Soviet forward observers could clearly see the Ferdinands, which were providing overwatch fire, and called down intense artillery barrages. One Borgward IV was hit by artillery, detonating its charge and destroying its nearby PzKpfw III control tank – part of which was flung up in the air and came down to disable one Ferdinand's main gun. Another Ferdinand was damaged by a direct artillery hit. Weidling, seeing the breaching attempt floundering, ordered a company of Ferdinands to move through the lanes and engage the nearest enemy strongpoints, in order to clear the way for his infantry. The heavy tank destroyers rumbled forward, detonating many mines, which disabled a good number of Ferdinands, but the rest were able to approach the Soviet positions. One Ferdinand hit five mines, but kept moving. The main problem was that the shock of mine explosions damaged the Ferdinand's two batteries, which were not shock-mounted in the hull. In a major oversight, Heeresgruppe Mitte had not requested replacement batteries for either the Ferdinands or the Tigers.

A Ferdinand from schwere Panzerjäger-Abteilung 653 that has suffered mine damage to its left front running gear. Replacing bent or broken roadwheel arms was a difficult and time-consuming task that could be done on the battlefield, and it was even more difficult when the necessary spare parts were not readily available. The magnificent Ferdinands arrived with virtually no logistic support package – a classic mistake with a new weapon that also plagued the introduction of the Panther in Heeresgruppe Süd. (Author's collection)

The 410th Rifle Regiment put up very tenacious resistance and managed to hold Weidling's heavily reinforced division at bay for most of the day, with one of its battalions suffering virtual annihilation. However, Grenadier-Regiment 184 managed to create a narrow gap between the Soviet regiment and its neighbour, 467th Rifle Regiment. By 1600 hours Grenadier-Regiment 184 and some Ferdinands had encircled the bulk of 467th Rifle Regiment and had compromised 81st Rifle Division's forward defences. As dusk approached, Barinov finally ordered both of his two hard-pressed frontline regiments to retreat to the division's second line of defence north of Ponyri, held by 519th Rifle Regiment. At considerable cost, Weidling's division managed to advance over 5km on the east side of the rail line and 3km on the west side, capturing Maloarkhangel'sk station. In order to prevent a German breakthrough on his corps' right flank, Slyshkin committed 27th Guards Tank Regiment, 129th Tank Brigade and 1442nd Self-Propelled Artillery Regiment – a total of 71 tanks and 16 Su-122s – to reinforce Barinov's battered division. Pukhov also directed his POZ (mobile obstacle) detachments to lay more mines in front of the German advance.

On Lemelsen's left flank, Generalleutnant Wolfgang von Kluge – younger brother of the Heeresgruppe Mitte commander – launched his 292.Infanterie-Division against the boundary between the Soviet 15th and 81st Rifle divisions, held by Polkovnik Nikolai Onoprienko's 676th Rifle Regiment. Kluge's division was supported by Panzerkompanie (Fkl) 314, which used a dozen Borgward IVs to blast three narrow lanes through the minefields east of Ozerki. Several PzKpfw III control tanks were able to move through these lanes without loss, but Soviet forward observers spotted the German breaching operation and brought down intense artillery concentrations on the cleared lanes, preventing dismounted pioneers from advancing to mark them out. Due to the heavy enemy fire, Kluge ordered the Ferdinands from schwere Panzerjäger-Abteilung 653 to move through the partly cleared lanes to suppress the enemy defences for his infantrymen. Although the buttoned-up crews within the Ferdinands were nearly invulnerable to the Soviet artillery fire, they were unable to see the cleared lane. As a result many wandered from the track and detonated anti-tank mines, which damaged their tracks and immobilized them. Once immobilized, the Ferdinand's lack of a turret and limited number of HE rounds carried made it difficult for them to provide effective fire support. Panzerkompanie (Fkl) 314 sent more Borgward IVs forward to widen the breach. One managed to roll into a trench filled with Soviet infantrymen, where it detonated. Now Kluge was forced to commit his infantry through the cleared lanes, despite the unsuppressed Soviet artillery. Eventually, 292.

A burning T-34 viewed through the rangefinder of a Ferdinand tank destroyer. Note that a Ferdinand is passing to the rear of the T-34. When used under favourable conditions, the Ferdinand and its powerful 8.8cm Pak 43/2 L/71 cannon could engage and destroy all current Soviet tanks from well beyond their ability to harm the Ferdinand. The Germans claimed that the two Ferdinand-equipped battalions knocked out a total of 502 Soviet tanks during the period between 5 and 27 July 1943. (Author's collection)

ATTACK OF THE FERDINANDS, 0700 HOURS, 5 JULY 1943 (PP. 42–43)

On the opening day of the *Zitadelle* offensive, the Germans made the mistake of using both battalions of Ferdinand tank destroyers to spearhead breakthrough attacks, even though the vehicle was totally unsuited for this role. Here a platoon of Ferdinands from Major Heinrich Steinwachs' schwere Panzerjäger-Abteilung 653 are used in support of 292.Infanterie-Division's attack near Veselyi Berezhoi. German pioneers used Borgward IV demolition carriers to blast a narrow corridor through the dense Soviet minefields, but this was only partly successful. Due to intense Soviet artillery and anti-tank fire at the breach site, the heavily armoured Ferdinands were ordered to move into the semi-cleared lane and assault the nearest enemy positions. Slowly, a platoon of four Ferdinands (**1**) waddles into the breach, which is obscured by dust and smoke from explosions and burning grass.

On the other side, a platoon of 76.2mm ZIS-3 anti-tank guns (**2**) pours fire at the approaching Ferdinands, while Soviet artillery plasters the entire area. The lead Ferdinand is hit repeatedly by 76.2mm shells, but they fail to penetrate its 200mm-thick frontal armour. However, one Ferdinand (**3**) wanders out of the cleared lane and detonates an anti-tank mine, which tears off its track and damages a roadwheel arm. The Ferdinands have no machine guns to engage the Soviet anti-tank guns, and their buttoned-up commanders (**4**) have difficulty spotting the AT guns (**5**) in the tall grass. Another Ferdinand (**6**) hits a mine but keeps on going, crushing barbed-wire obstacles (**7**) in its path. Meanwhile, German artillery fire is taking its toll on the exposed anti-tank guns, with one piece knocked out (**8**) and several crew members down. Eventually, enough of the Ferdinands survive to push through the breach, encouraging the German infantry to follow – but this type of assault soon incapacitates more than half of the Ferdinands.

Infanterie-Division was able to fight its way through these outer defences, but at great cost. Moreover, schwere Panzerjäger-Abteilung 653 only had 12 out of 45 Ferdinands still operational by the day's end.

Once 292.Infanterie-Division had weakened the right flank of 15th Rifle Division, Lemelsen slowly committed Generalmajor Karl-Wilhelm von Schlieben's 18.Panzer-Division and Sturmpanzer-Abteilung 216 into battle to complete the encirclement of 676th Rifle Regiment. Schlieben's division was primarily structured as a mechanized infantry support and exploitation force, and advanced in two groups: Kampfgruppe von Seydlitz and Kampfgruppe Fleischauer. This force was better suited to engaging infantry targets than the Ferdinands, since in addition to the Sturmpanzers it had PzKpfw III Ausf. N tanks equipped with 7.5cm howitzers and Panzer-Artillerie Regiment 88. Schlieben's armour advanced cautiously through the partly cleared mines, losing some tanks, but ultimately flanking Onoprienko's 676th Rifle Regiment by 1000 hours. Onoprienko was forced to pull his regiment into a tight hedgehog, deployed for all-around defence.

On Lemelsen's right flank, Harpe's XXXXI Panzerkorps launched its attack initially with just 6.Infanterie-Division at 0630 hours, although Generalmajor Mortimer von Kessel's 20.Panzer-Division joined in at 0800 hours. Engineers from Pionier-Bataillon 6 were forced to clear lanes through the enemy minefields in broad daylight, but Soviet artillery fire was weak in this sector due to the unusually effective German artillery preparation, which had disrupted wire

During the assault on 5 July, Soviet artillery detonated several of the Borgward IV demolition carriers. Here, a Borgward IV detonated (centre) and destroyed its PzKpfw III control tank (left) and damaged another (right). The turret was blown off the PzKpfw III at left and it struck a nearby Ferdinand, knocking out its main gun. Note the Ferdinand in the background. (Author's collection)

A PzKpfw IV medium tank with *Schürzen* side skirts during the opening days of *Zitadelle*. By mid-1943, the improved PzKpfw IV models had finally gained the ability to reliably defeat the T-34, but their battlefield life was increasingly at risk from improved Soviet anti-tank defences. Although AOK 9 only lost 35 PzKpfw IV tanks as 'totally destroyed' during *Zitadelle*, many more were rendered non-operational due to battle damage. (Ian Barter)

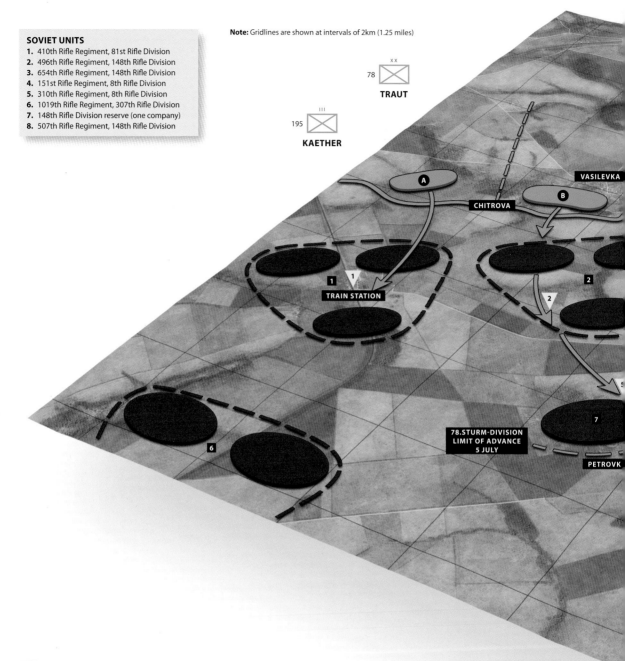

SOVIET UNITS
1. 410th Rifle Regiment, 81st Rifle Division
2. 496th Rifle Regiment, 148th Rifle Division
3. 654th Rifle Regiment, 148th Rifle Division
4. 151st Rifle Regiment, 8th Rifle Division
5. 310th Rifle Regiment, 8th Rifle Division
6. 1019th Rifle Regiment, 307th Rifle Division
7. 148th Rifle Division reserve (one company)
8. 507th Rifle Regiment, 148th Rifle Division

Note: Gridlines are shown at intervals of 2km (1.25 miles)

78 ⊠ TRAUT

195 ⊠ KAETHER

A

B

VASILEVKA

CHITROVA

1

TRAIN STATION

2

2

78.STURM-DIVISION
LIMIT OF ADVANCE
5 JULY

7

PETROVK

6

▼ EVENTS

Events

1. 0600 hours, 5 July: Grenadier-Regiment 216 launches its attack, supported by Ferdinand tank destroyers and assault guns. After great difficulty fighting through mines and 410th Rifle Regiment, this group reaches Maloarkhangel'sk train station by dusk.

2. 0600 hours, 5 July: Oberstleutnant Holländer's Sturm-Regiment 195 attacks the western battalion of 496th Rifle Regiment and manages to overrun part of the position, thanks to a heavy barrage from Nebelwerfers and 12cm mortars.

3. 0600 hours, 5 July: Oberst Kaether's Sturm-Regiment 14 attacks toward Trosna and manages to penetrate between 496th and 654th Rifle regiments.

4. 0600 hours, 5 July: one battalion of Major Klocke's Sturm-Regiment 215 (the other battalion remains in division reserve) attacks toward Mayskaya Zorka, but is repulsed.

5. Afternoon, 5 July: when 496th Rifle Regiment is threatened with encirclement, its troops begin withdrawing towards 148th Rifle Division's second echelon positions at Protasovo. Sturm-Regiment 195 pursues, and reaches the outskirts of Petrovka by evening.

6. Morning–afternoon, 5 July: the two regiments of 216.Infanterie-Division conduct several attacks throughout the day against 8th Rifle Division, but make only minimal gains.

THE ATTACK OF 78.STURM-DIVISION, 5 JULY 1943

The Germans had carefully rebuilt 78.Infanterie-Division as a specialized assault formation, and provided it with a wealth of infantry support weapons. The failure of this division to achieve its objectives on the first day of *Zitadelle* denied XXIII Armeekorps any hope of seizing Maloarkhangel'sk.

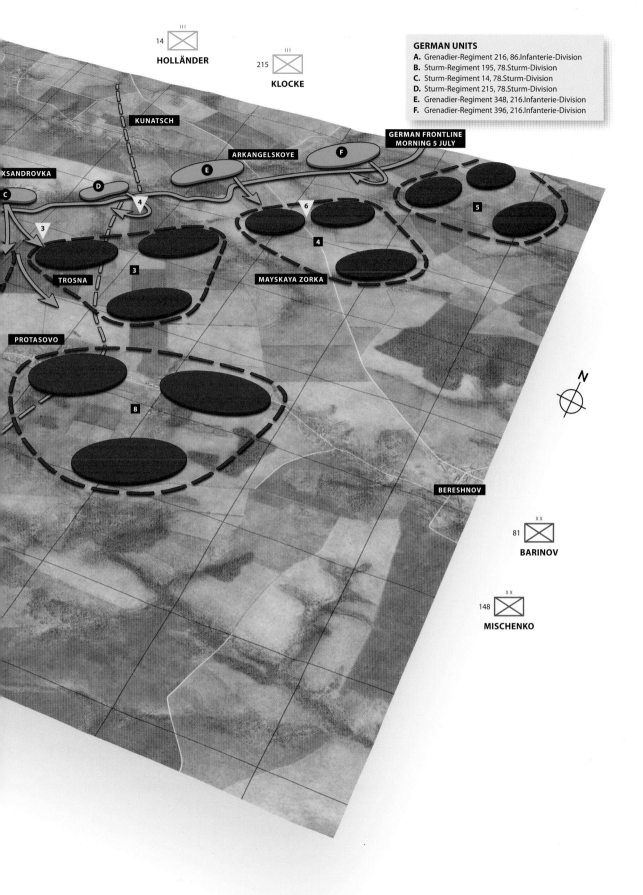

14 HOLLÄNDER

215 KLOCKE

KUNATSCH

GERMAN FRONTLINE
MORNING 5 JULY

ARKANGELSKOYE

F

E

XSANDROVKA

D

C

4

3

TROSNA

6

4

MAYSKAYA ZORKA

5

PROTASOVO

8

BERESHNOV

81 BARINOV

148 MISCHENKO

47

A battery of Soviet 122mm M-30 howitzers, dug in on a hillside and camouflaged. While Soviet artillery posed little direct threat to German tanks, their heavy shells could destroy German SPW half-tracks and other light vehicles in the German kampfgruppen. Again and again, massed Soviet artillery prevented the Germans from achieving real mass on the battlefield. (From the fonds of the RGAKFD in Krasnogorsk via Stavka)

communications to forward observers. After two hours, the pioneers were finally able to clear sufficient lanes for the assault troops to advance. They proceeded to attack the forward strongpoints of 47th Rifle Regiment south of the Oka River, near Yasnaya Polyana. Pukhov later claimed that there were flaws in the layout of 15th Rifle Division's forward defences, which had been noted – but not corrected – prior to *Zitadelle*. This sounds suspiciously like an *ex post facto* rationalization of his own faulty battle command. Polkovnik Ivan Kartashev's 47th Rifle Regiment had been hit particularly hard by the German air and artillery bombardment, which knocked out two-thirds of its anti-tank guns and severed wire communications to Dzhandzhgava's divisional command post. Kartashev's regiment was still disrupted when the assault elements of 6.Infanterie-Division began attacking his forward battalion strongpoints around 0900 hours. A kampfgruppe from 20.Panzer-Division supported the attack against Kartashev's left flank, which struck Kapitan N. A. Rakitsky's 2nd Battalion; German tanks and Schützenpanzerwagen (SPWs) approached through deadspace in a ravine that was apparently not well covered either by obstacles or fire, and quickly overran the Soviet battalion. Rakitsky's battalion broke and survivors bolted for the rear. Kartashev tried to restore the situation by launching an immediate counterattack with his 1st Battalion, but this effort was repulsed and these defeated troops also retreated without order. Motorized troops from 20.Panzer-Division poured into the gap, exploiting the Soviet retreat. Meanwhile Major Sauvant's Tiger tanks (schwere Panzer-Abteilung 505) came through gaps in the minefields created by Borgward IV demolition vehicles near Yasnaya Polyana and struck the right flank of the crumbling 47th Rifle Regiment. Only the 3rd Battalion/47th Rifle Regiment, under Kapitan N.D. Zhukov, managed to hold its position, which was reinforced by 12 ZIS-3 76.2mm anti-tank guns.

Major Sauvant's Tigers (of which six had been damaged by mines) opted to bypass Zhukov's encircled strongpoint, letting 6.Infanterie-Division mop them up. Sauvant focused on pressing south towards Podolyan, seeking to overrun 15th Rifle Division's second echelon positions before the Soviets recovered their balance. Pukhov was surprised by the sudden collapse of 15th Rifle Division's left flank and ordered 237th Tank Regiment and 1441st Self-Propelled Artillery Regiment to move immediately to Soborovka to block the German armour.

Meanwhile, the broken troops from 47th Rifle Regiment retreated south to Soborovka, through the positions of Polkovnik Aleksandr T. Prokopenko's 321st Rifle Regiment, with German panzers and panzergrenadiers hard on their heels. 20.Panzer-Division captured Podolyan against feeble resistance. Two small combined-arms kampfgruppen attacked Prokopenko's positions, which were also in danger of envelopment by 1100 hours. However, Lemelsen opted to bypass Prokopenko's regiment and continue south as far as possible. Generalmajor von Kessel, leading 20.Panzer-Division, was an odd choice to form the tip of the spear since he had been head of the Army's Personnel Department between 1939 and 1942 and had no recent command or combat experience – hardly one of the 'best commanders' that Hitler had envisioned in the *Zitadelle* plan. At any rate, 20.Panzer-Division succeeded in achieving the biggest German coup of the first day by capturing the village of Soborovka. Two tank companies and some panzergrenadiers approached Soborovka at 1800 hours. Although the village was an anti-tank strongpoint with five well-camouflaged anti-tank guns, a combined-arms attack from two directions quickly overran the village. The capture of Soborovka marked the deepest German penetration on the first day of *Zitadelle* – a total of 8km.

On the western end of AOK 9's designated breakthrough zone, General der Infanterie Hans Zorn's XXXXVI Panzerkorps attacked the right flank of the Soviet 70th Army with the 7., 31. and 258. Infantry divisions at 0634 hours. The main effort was made by Generalleutnant Friedrich Hoßbach's 31.Infanterie-Division, which attempted to seize high ground around Tureika and Gnilets, held by General-Major Timofei K. Shkrylev's 132nd Rifle Division. After advancing 3km in three hours, Hoßbach's division encountered heavy resistance at Hill 244.9. Kluge and Luftflotte 6's Ritter von Greim arrived at Zorn's command post to watch the beginning of the offensive. Greim organized an attack by two complete Stuka groups against Hill 244.9, but this did not occur until 1240 hours. Eventually, German firepower forced the 132nd Rifle Division to abandon Hill 244.9 by 1615 hours. The 7.Infanterie-Division advanced barely 2km and failed to capture Tureika. Likewise, 258.Infanterie-Division's attacks barely dented the Soviet outpost lines and Stossgruppe von Manteuffel did little more than screen the corps' right flank. Zorn's attack, which cost his corps at least 1,444 casualties, failed to secure the key terrain that it was expected to on the first day of *Zitadelle*; nor did it penetrate 70th Army's first line of defence.

Meanwhile, the air battle over the northern battlefield on 5 July was dominated by the Luftwaffe. General-Leytenant Sergei I. Rudenko, commander of 16th Air Army, made the mistake of committing his fighters piece-meal, which led to very heavy losses in the skies over Maloarkhangel'sk. The Fw-190 pilots had a field day, shooting down small groups of Soviet fighters as they appeared, as well as unescorted Il-2 Sturmoviks. Rokossovsky was appalled by the Luftwaffe's apparent dominance over the battlefield, and at 0930 hours ordered Rudenko to commit 200 fighters to regain air control and 200 bombers to attack the German spearheads hitting Pukhov's army. Although the Soviet bombers were able to conduct some effective attacks against German armoured concentrations, their fighters were unable to gain control of the air. During the course of the day, 1.Flieger-Division flew 2,088 sorties and lost 25 aircraft (11 fighters, 8 Stukas and 6 bombers), while 16th Air Army flew 1,720 sorties and lost 100 aircraft (83 fighters, 16 Sturmoviks and 1 bomber). Clearly, the Luftwaffe achieved a significant victory over the northern sector of the Kursk salient on the first day of *Zitadelle*.

A German PzKpfw III Ausf. L medium tank that has been immobilized by mine damage is shelled repeatedly by Soviet artillery. Under these conditions battlefield recovery was impossible and the tank would be abandoned, even though the damage was repairable. Given their inadequate firepower and armoured protection, the PzKpfw IIIs played only a supporting role during *Zitadelle*. (Courtesy of the Central Museum of the Armed Forces, Moscow via Stavka)

A German SdKfz 251/10 SPW half-track knocked out, probably by mines. This variant of the Schützenpanzerwagen was equipped with a 3.7cm Pak gun, which could provide fire support to a panzergrenadier platoon. Each panzer division in 1943 usually had one Panzergrenadier batallion equipped with SPWs, but the other three battalions still rode in trucks. During *Zitadelle*, only the SPW-equipped battalions could keep up with the panzers. (Courtesy of the Central Museum of the Armed Forces, Moscow via Stavka)

By afternoon, Model was sufficiently satisfied with the day's progress to order Harpe to bring up his 2. and 9. Panzer divisions. The Germans had seen very little of Rokossovsky's armour on the first day of *Zitadelle*, but Model expected that 2nd Tank Army would be committed when AOK 9 began to attack the second line of defence; he wanted his best panzer units on hand when that occurred. The lead elements of 2. and 9. Panzer divisions reached the forward edge of the battle area by late afternoon and were ready to spearhead the assault on the second day. Despite mine and artillery damage to a significant number of armoured vehicles, AOK 9 had not lost a great deal of its armour on the first day of *Zitadelle* – contrary to exaggerated Soviet claims about knocking out 200 German tanks. Soviet anti-tank mines greatly slowed the German advance and damaged many vehicles, but they could not destroy tanks. Instead, they knocked off tracks and damaged road-wheel arms, which could be replaced in a matter of hours. The problem was that AOK 9 began *Zitadelle* with a serious shortage of spare parts and could only keep its armour running through the self-defeating practice of cannibalization (stripping parts from one damaged vehicle to repair another). This process could only sustain combat losses for a few days. Losses among the German infantry and pioneers were more serious. The AOK 9 suffered 7,223 casualties on the first day of *Zitadelle*, including 1,301 dead or missing; three-quarters of these casualties were in the infantry divisions. With no infantry divisions in reserve to reinforce the attack, Model could see that his infantry strength would likely be exhausted before he had defeated Rokossovsky's best units.

A Tiger rearming in the field. Refuelling and rearming was (and still is) a vital component in armoured operations and even minor disruptions could cause tanks to be sidelined for vital hours. (Bundesarchiv, Bild 101I-022-2948-23)

Rokossovsky was not satisfied with the results of the first day, due to the rapid loss of 13th Army's first line of defence and 16th Air Army's inability to gain control of the airspace. During the night, the battered 29th Rifle Corps – including Polkovnik Onoprienko's 676th Rifle Regiment – abandoned its remaining first-line positions and fell back to the second line between Samodurovka and Ponyri. Dzhandzhgava's 15th Rifle Division was combat ineffective after losing 1,840 men and 80 pieces, and Barinov's 81st Rifle Division was in equally poor shape.

Rokossovsky was being constantly pestered by Zhukov and Stavka for information about the course of the battle, so simply remaining on the defence seemed a risky course of action to him. He still remembered having his teeth smashed out by the NKVD while in prison and had no intention of giving Stalin a chance to condemn him for inactivity. Consequently, Rokossovsky decided to mount a major counterattack with virtually all his armour on 6 July, to restore the frontline. He intended to use not only the separate 19th Tank Corps, but 3rd and 16th Tank corps from Rodin's 2nd Tank Army as well. This was a poor decision, not in accord with Soviet defensive planning for the battle, and it played directly into Model's hands. Soviet armour was not supposed to be committed to battle until the panzers had been significantly worn down by losses from mines and anti-tank guns, which had not yet occurred.

German infantry watch their artillery pound a Soviet position. Due to the loss of so many junior officers and NCOs between 1941 and 1942, the German infantry no longer had much stomach for offensive action – particularly across open terrain in daylight. Heavy losses in the first days of *Zitadelle* further dampened their offensive ardour. Instead, the German infantry tended to wait for their artillery and the Luftwaffe to clear the way, which reduced advances to only a few kilometres per day. (Ian Barter)

A crewman examines a shell hit on the Tiger's side armour, which failed to penetrate. The Tigers were hit repeatedly, and even without penetration the shock could damage components inside the vehicle such as the optical sights, the radio and the batteries. Despite the accumulation of battle damage, the morale of Tiger crews rose as they realized that they were much safer than their compatriots in the medium tanks. (Bundesarchiv, Bild 101I-022-2935-25A)

6 JULY

The second day of *Zitadelle* began heavily overcast, and scattered showers followed throughout the day. Rokossovsky's forces made the first move, with an artillery counter-barrage by Ignatov's 4th Artillery Corps against the spearheads of XXXXVII Panzerkorps around Podolyan at 0450 hours. This was followed by a raid of 25 A-20 bombers from 221st Bomber Aviation Division, which successfully bombed 2.Panzer-Division. None of Model's forces were ready to resume the offensive at first light and spent the early morning hours re-organizing and bringing up second-echelon forces. Model decided that only Lemelsen's and Harpe's corps would conduct major attacks on the second day, but he directed the other two corps on the flanks to mount limited-objective operations to secure the objectives that should have been taken on the first day. In the XXXXVI Panzerkorps sector, 31.Infanterie-Division captured the town of Gnilets at 0910 hours, but any further advance to the south was thwarted by thick belts of mines and infantry strongpoints. In the XXIII Armeekorps sector in the east, 78.Sturm-Division, supported by 12 Ferdinands and 19 assault guns, attacked Hill 253.5. Progress on both of AOK 9's flanks was limited.

Rokossovsky wanted General-Leytenant Aleksei G. Rodin's 2nd Tank Army to counterattack the German spearhead at dawn with 16th and 19th Tank corps, but this was simply too rushed. Instead, Rodin was only able to get General-Major Vasily E. Grigor'ev's 16th Tank Corps into action during the morning. The corps had to make a forward passage of lines through the Soviet 17th Guards Rifle Corps' positions in Pukhov's second line of defence; this took time. It was not until 1040 hours that Grigor'ev could begin his attack, and even then it was a piece-meal effort with just the 107th and 164th Tank brigades. Fewer than 100 tanks were committed to the counterattack, which went in without reconnaissance or proper artillery support. Near the village of Bobrik Major Sauvant's Tigers were waiting and easily spotted the approaching Soviet armour, which had to cross several kilometres of open ground. Taking advantage of perfect firing conditions, Sauvant's Tigers began engaging the Soviet tanks well outside the effective range of the T-34's main gun. Polkovnik Nikolai M. Teliakov, a highly experienced tanker, led his 107th Tank Brigade forward resolutely, but 46 of his tanks were knocked out. The Soviet 164th Tank Brigade tried to avoid Sauvant's Tigers, but instead ran into the lead elements of 2.Panzer-Division, losing 23 tanks as a result. Although 16th Tank Corps' losses were heavy, they managed to get close enough to knock out 10 German tanks. After these two Soviet brigades were repulsed, Rodin broke off the attack and opted to regroup his remaining armour around the village of Snova. This was the kind of action that embellished the Tiger's lethal reputation on both sides.

Soviet infantry counterattack into a village, rushing past a knocked-out German StuG III. Rokossovsky's forces conducted a very active defence around Ponyri, Ol'khovatka and Teploye, mounting frequent counterattacks that made it difficult for the Germans to consolidate their gains. (From the fonds of the RGAKFD in Krasnogorsk via Stavka)

The second day of *Zitadelle* and the Soviet reactions, 6 July 1943.

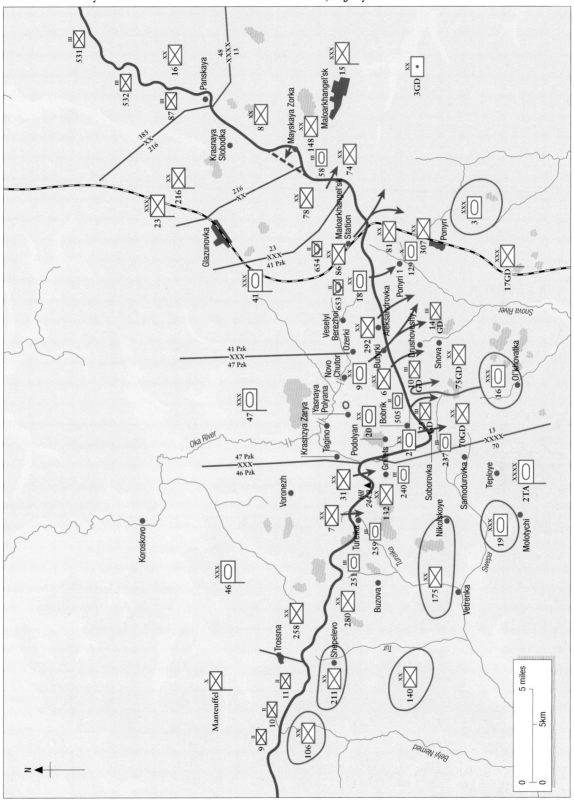

Rudenko's 16th Air Army was far more aggressive on the second day of *Zitadelle* and tried to employ attacks by massed formations of Il-2 Sturmoviks to break up the German panzer concentrations. However, coordination between Soviet fighters and ground attack units was still inadequate; when 2nd Guards Ground Attack Aviation Division tried to attack, it was pounced on by Fw-190 fighters from Jagdgeschwader 51, which shot down 15 Il-2s. Another attack by 299th Ground Attack Aviation Division at 0700 hours was more successful, losing only one Il-2. Later in the morning Luftflotte 6 committed its own ground attack assets to support the advance of Lemelsen's XXXXVII Panzerkorps; Rudenko committed his fighters to prevent this, but the German fighters again inflicted disproportionate losses on their opponents. Despite 16th Air Army flying over 1,000 sorties and fuel shortages beginning to affect its operations, Luftflotte 6 was able to maintain air superiority over the critical sectors during the day. Overall, the German pilots managed to shoot down 91 Soviet aircraft for the loss of only 11 of their own. In just two days of combat, the Soviet 6th Fighter Corps had been reduced from 110 to 48 fighters.

Once Rodin's premature counterattack had been dealt with, and the Luftwaffe had gained firm control of the air over the northern sector, Model resumed AOK 9's offensive around noon. His intent was to breach Pukhov's second line of defence between Samodurovka and Ponyri, held by 17th Guards Rifle Corps. However, AOK 9 had no real *schwerpunkt* on 6 July. Instead, 2.Panzer-Division and Sauvant's Tigers pushed south toward Ol'khovatka, while 20.Panzer-Division protected the western flank against local counterattacks from 70th Army. In the centre, 9.Panzer-Division and 6. and 292. Infantry divisions pushed toward the Snova River valley. However, Harpe's XXXXI Panzerkorps did not make a direct push for Ponyri, but instead directed 18.Panzer-Division and 86.Infanterie-Division to first roll up the remnants of Barinov's 81st Rifle Division north of the town. Barinov's division lost 2,518 troops in the first two days of *Zitadelle* and was near collapse. Pukhov was able to rush General-Major Mikhail A. Enshin's 307th Rifle Division and Polkovnik Nikolai V. Petrushin's 129th Tank Brigade to hold Ponyri. Enshin had just taken over the division, but he was a rock-solid NKVD officer who could be trusted to hold this critical position.

Harpe's forces advanced cautiously against Barinov's 81st Rifle Division, which mounted furious local counterattacks. On this day the German armour was in the lead, with the infantry and pioneers assigned a supporting role. One group of Ferdinands from schwere Panzerjäger-Abteilung 653, advancing with 292.Infanterie-Division, sparred with T-34s from Petrushin's brigade, but then unexpectedly met their match. Pukhov had also sent 1442nd Self-Propelled Artillery Regiment to Ponyri, and its Su-152s

The Steyr-built Raupenschlepper Ost (RSO) tracked vehicle began reaching the Eastern Front in late 1942, and finally provided the German Army with a prime mover that could traverse the difficult terrain in Russia. Several of the elite units in AOK 9 were equipped with the RSO, including the 12cm mortar battalions. (Bundesarchiv, Bild 101I-154-1990-35A)

engaged the Ferdinands. Although the Soviets later claimed many Ferdinands and Tigers were destroyed by Su-152s, on this occasion at least one Ferdinand was knocked out by an Su-152 with a flank shot from 800m. Barinov's resistance slowed Harpe's advance, but did not stop it; by 1700 hours 18.Panzer-Division and a dozen Ferdinands were on the northern outskirts of Ponyri. However, by then 3rd Tank Corps and a great deal of artillery had arrived just south of the town. As evening approached, Pukhov allowed Barinov's battered division – which had lost 2,518 out of its 8,000 men – to withdraw to the rear and hand over the battle to Enshin's fresh division. Enshin enjoyed a wealth of support, including the entire 5th Breakthrough Artillery Division, two brigades of multiple rocket launchers and 13th Anti-Tank Brigade. As David Glantz noted (1986, p. 53), 'the 380-gun support for the 307th Rifle Division was the largest amount of artillery put at the disposal of a single rifle division on the defence in the entire war in the east'.

In order to outflank the tough Soviet defences north of Ponyri, Generalleutnant Walter Scheller's 9.Panzer-Division slashed cross-country with Kampfgruppe Mummert and Kampfgruppe Schmahl towards the Snova River, approaching Ponyri from the north-west. Yet this advance presented the remainder of Grigor'ev's 16th Tank Corps, concentrated around the village of Snova, with an excellent opportunity to harass Kampfgruppe Schmahl with enfilade fire, inflicting some losses. By 2215 hours Scheller's division had established a bridgehead across the Snova River and was near the western approaches to Ponyri. While Harpe succeeded in eliminating the remainder of Pukhov's first line of defence in his sector by the end of the second day of *Zitadelle*, he had barely scratched the second line of defence anchored on Ponyri, which was much stronger.

Lemelsen's XXXXVII Panzerkorps advanced southwards toward Ol'khovatka with Generalleutnant Vollrath Lübbe's 2.Panzer-Division in the lead and Major Sauvant's Tigers in support. General-Leytenant Andrei L. Bondarev's 17th Guards Rifle Corps was squarely in Lemelsen's path, with 6th, 70th and 75th Guards Rifle divisions. Lübbe's division was probably the best panzer unit in AOK 9, but it was confronted with previously unknown minefields (some of which had been recently laid by POZ units) and even thicker anti-tank defences than it had found in the first line of defence. The Soviet 76.2mm ZIS-3 anti-tank guns were extremely difficult to spot in the tall grass from more than a few hundred metres, since with even modest entrenchment their profile could be lowered to less than 1m high. In contrast, the German tanks were over 2.6m in height; this meant that the Soviet anti-tank guns usually got the first shot in. Soviet tanks from 2nd Tank Army were also in the vicinity and continued to snipe at the flanks of the German advance.

While 6th Guards Rifle Division – which was spread across a very wide front – was slowly ground up by the German attack, the German armour began to suffer from the

Su-76M assault guns moving up to the front. The Su-76M was introduced in early 1943 and featured the ZIS-3 anti-tank gun mounted on the hull of a T-70 light tank. Although still only available in small numbers in July 1943, the Su-76M was an excellent infantry support weapon. (From the fonds of the RGAKFD in Krasnogorsk via Stavka)

The Red Army was impressed by the utility of German assault guns and decided to develop the Su-122, which combined a 122mm M-30 howitzer atop a T-34 hull. The Su-122 first appeared in December 1942, but by July 1943 Rokossovsky still only had a few regiments of these weapons. The Su-122 was not a major success during the battle of Kursk, but it proved more useful afterwards in reducing German strongpoints during AOK 9's retreat to the Hagen Stellung. (Author's collection)

combination of Soviet artillery fire, anti-tank guns and mines. Major Sauvant's Tigers had a bad day, with 12 Tigers suffering mine damage; schwere Panzer-Abteilung 505's repair group lacked sufficient spare parts to repair more than a handful by that evening. With more than half its Tigers out of action, Heeresgruppe Mitte made an emergency request for 10 new Tiger transmissions, more engines and more road-wheel arms, but none were available in Russia. Instead, the critical parts had to be flown directly from the Henschel plant in Kassel. This was no way to run an offensive. Although 2.Panzer-Division also lost a number of tanks, it managed to bull its way forward through 6th Guards Rifle Division. Soviet air attacks and artillery fire were intense in this area, and even Lemelsen was wounded, albeit lightly. By late afternoon XXXXVII Panzerkorps had run up against 70th and 75th Guards Rifle divisions and was halted. At 1730 hours General-Major Ivan D. Vasil'ev's 19th Tank Corps launched an attack against Lemelsen's right flank, which initially caught 20.Panzer-Division by surprise. With the help of close air support from Luftflotte 6, 20.Panzer-Division was able to repulse Vasil'ev's armour and knock out thirty T-34s and one Su-76.

The second day of *Zitadelle* had been disappointing for AOK 9. It suffered 2,996 casualties, including 645 dead or missing, but achieved only modest advances of 2 to 4km. Model was unwilling to commit his armour against the Soviet strongpoint at Ponyri. He ordered Harpe to shift 9. and 18. Panzer divisions to the defence, and would try to take the town the next day with 86. and 292. Infantry divisions. Although Pukhov's second line of defence had barely been dented, Model also decided to start feeding Gruppe Esbeck, his main mobile reserve, into the battle. He decided to commit 4.Panzer-Division to support a renewed advance by Lemelsen's corps. A kampfgruppe from 12.Panzer-Division was also brought up.

An SdKfz 250/5 artillery observation half-track from 2. Panzer-Division's artillery regiment passes an abandoned Soviet 76.2mm ZIS-3 gun while advancing south towards Ol'khovatka. Given that the Soviet weapon is in a towed configuration, the weapon was probably being withdrawn during the retreat of 15th Rifle Division. (Author's collection)

Two knocked-out T-34s. Although Rokossovsky's Central Front lost hundreds of tanks during *Zitadelle*, its overall losses in armour were no more than 30 per-cent of its strength; Model failed in his objective of incapacitating Rodin's 2nd Tank Army. Furthermore, the Soviets held the battlefield, and many knocked-out tanks were recovered and repaired. (Author's collection)

7 JULY

Model was resolved to breach the Soviet second line of defence on the third day of battle, before his strained material and human resources gave out. He also recognized that the supporting attacks on the flanks by XXIII Armeekorps and XXXXVI Panzerkorps were not going to accomplish much more, but might still serve a diversionary function, so he directed them to continue small-scale attacks. He decided to narrow his focus and concentrate his firepower against the Soviet strongpoints at Ponyri and Ol'khovatka; if these could be taken, Rokossovsky's second line might still be overcome.

The weather was much improved on the third day and air operations on both sides began early. Reinforced by two batteries of assault guns and the remaining Ferdinands of schwere Panzerjäger-Abteilung 653, 292.Infanterie-Division attacked at 0630 hours with two regiments into the north-western outskirts of Ponyri, which was held by 1019th Rifle Regiment. Overnight the corps-level POZ had laid more mines in front of Enshin's perimeter and the German armour ran into them, disabling many vehicles. Enshin unleashed his artillery as the Germans were tangled up in the mines, firing barrages of Katyusha rockets and tube artillery at the enemy. The ground heaved under the weight of metal and the German attack was repulsed. After regrouping for an hour, 292.Infanterie-Division tried again, but with similar results. Harpe tried to get 18.Panzer-Division into the fight by creating a crossing site over the Snova to mount an enveloping attack against the west side of the town, but this was also disrupted by Soviet artillery fire. Rudenko's 16th Air Army, learning from previous mistakes, succeeded in

A squadron of Yak-9T fighters lined up prior to *Zitadelle*. The 20mm ShVAK cannon is prominent in the nose. 16th Air Army had several regiments equipped with the Yak-9T and they were put to good use in harassing German logistical traffic just behind the front. (Courtesy of the Central Museum of the Armed Forces, Moscow via Stavka)

getting its Il-2s and Pe-2s through the German fighter screen to pound the German assault groups north of Ponyri, further adding to Harpe's difficulty. By 1030 hours Enshin's division had repulsed four German attacks and lost no ground.

Stymied by 1019th Rifle Regiment, Harpe brought Weidling's 86. Infanterie-Division up to mount a supporting attack against Enshin's right flank around 1100 hours.

Two knocked-out, US-made M3 Lee tanks. Even in the third year of the war, the Red Army was still forced to use inferior Lend-Lease tanks, since Soviet industry could not yet build enough T-34s to equip all tank brigades. The M3's high profile and limited mobility made it poorly suited to the conditions at Kursk, and they suffered heavy losses whenever committed to action against German armour. (Author's collection)

Weidling's infantry and assault guns managed to capture a small feature, Hill 257.1, east of Ponyri – which succeeded in diverting much of the artillery supporting 1019th Rifle Regiment's defence. Once the volume of defensive fire was reduced north of Ponyri, 292.Infanterie-Division made another attack against 1019th Rifle Regiment around noon. This time the Soviet regiment buckled and the German troops managed to fight their way into the northern part of Ponyri. Enshin was forced to commit two battalions from his second-echelon 1023rd Rifle Regiment and Petrushin's T-34s to mount an immediate counterattack to prevent the loss of Ponyri. Nevertheless, some German troops were able to reach the train station. The next five hours were spent in close-quarters city fighting, until evening approached. Harpe's troops managed to hold on to the northern part of Ponyri, but 292.Infanterie-Division suffered very heavy losses. 18.Panzer-Division finally succeeded in getting a few companies of panzers and panzergrenadiers across the Snova to capture Hill 240.2 on the west side of Ponyri by 2100 hours. Nevertheless, the Soviet artillery completely dominated the battlefield around Ponyri, harassing any sign of movement or troop concentrations with intense barrages. Harpe's XXXXI Panzerkorps had gained very little ground. Indeed, the idea of an entire German Panzerkorps being committed to capture a single small town – and failing – appeared ludicrous.

In an effort to assist Harpe in outflanking the Soviet strongpoint at Ponyri, Lemelsen sent Scheller's 9.Panzer-Division from the village of Rzhavets (4km west of Ponyri) to attack southwards towards Bityug, where there was a small bridge over the Snova. However, the Soviets had anticipated this move. As a consequence, Scheller's vanguard, Kampfgruppe Schmahl, ran into dense minefields and intense anti-tank fire, which resulted in Panzer-Regiment 33 losing two PzKpfw IV tanks destroyed and two PzKpfw III and five PzKpfw IV damaged. Already, a variety of mechanical defects had temporarily cost Scheller 40 of his tanks, and the German logistic units failed to push spare parts forward in a timely manner. Kampfgruppe Schulz pushed on with just 12 tanks and two companies of panzergrenadiers mounted in SPWs, reaching Bityug around 1900 hours. By day's end, Scheller's 9.Panzer-Division had suffered significant losses and accomplished only a 3km advance with a token force.

In one of the bizarre incidents of war, 78.Sturm-Division requested that two Ferdinands be attached to its forward units to help it hold an exposed position. However, after the Ferdinands had reached the position, the local infantry unit decided to pull back anyway during the night – without informing the Ferdinands' crews. During the night Soviet infantry captured one Ferdinand intact when its sleepy crew was surprised. The other Ferdinand attempted to flee but became stuck in a ditch and was abandoned. These two intact Ferdinands featured prominently in Soviet propaganda about the battle, although their loss was purely accidental.

Lemelsen's XXXXVII Panzerkorps intended to make its main effort towards Ol'khovatka with Lübbe's 2.Panzer-Division and Major Sauvant's remaining Tigers, while Kessel's 20.Panzer-Division launched a supporting attack to complete the capture of Samodurovka and gain some elbow room. Noticeably, Lemelsen was relying entirely on his armour and had pulled 6. Infanterie-Division out of the frontline to regroup. Lübbe's spearhead was Kampfgruppe Burmeister, consisting of Panzer-Regiment 3, a battalion of panzergrenadiers in SPWs, reconnaissance, self-propelled artillery and panzerjägers – a very powerful force. Oberst Arnold Burmeister, a very experienced soldier, was in charge of this battering ram. Yet an armoured concentration of this size was impossible to conceal; an early-morning raid by Soviet A-20 bombers caught Kampfgruppe Burmeister by surprise, and destroyed five PzKpfw IV tanks. After recovering from this attack, Kampfgruppe Burmeister moved south-west and struck 140th Rifle Division's positions on Hill 220, near Samodurovka. This position was overrun and Burmeister claimed to have knocked out 15 Soviet tanks. However, he apparently lacked

A German panzer kampfgruppe moves through an open area under heavy artillery bombardment. Note that although all the German tanks have open hatches, the commanders have ducked down inside. The German tanks appear to roughly be in an arrowhead formation, but no support vehicles are in sight – they are further back. Despite frequent descriptions of Kursk as a massive tank battle involving hundreds of tanks, this was the reality at the tip of the spear – individual tank companies trying to fight their way through dense defences. (Süd-Deutsch Zeitung, 127124)

The 76.2mm ZIS-3 or 'crash-boom' anti-tank gun. Note that the gun is barely higher than the adjacent tall grass, which would have made it very difficult to spot from more than 300m away. Usually the Soviet anti-tank gunners would get the first shot in. (From the fonds of the RGAKFD in Krasnogorsk via Stavka)

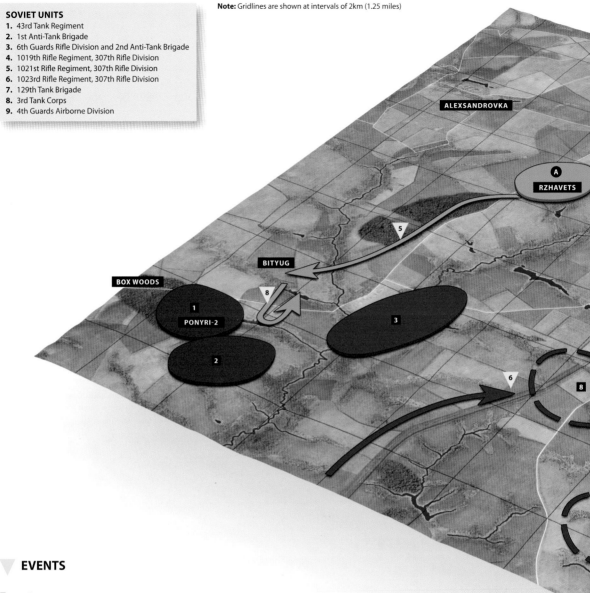

SOVIET UNITS
1. 43rd Tank Regiment
2. 1st Anti-Tank Brigade
3. 6th Guards Rifle Division and 2nd Anti-Tank Brigade
4. 1019th Rifle Regiment, 307th Rifle Division
5. 1021st Rifle Regiment, 307th Rifle Division
6. 1023rd Rifle Regiment, 307th Rifle Division
7. 129th Tank Brigade
8. 3rd Tank Corps
9. 4th Guards Airborne Division

Note: Gridlines are shown at intervals of 2km (1.25 miles)

ALEXSANDROVKA

RZHAVETS

BITYUG

BOX WOODS

PONYRI-2

▽ EVENTS

Events

1. 0630 hours, 7 July: reinforced by two batteries of assault guns and Sturmpanzers, 292.Infanterie-Division attacks into the northern outskirts of Ponyri. It is repulsed by Enshin's 307th Rifle Division, supported by over 300 artillery pieces.

2. 7 July: 18.Panzer-Division attempts to create a crossing over the Snova to enable an attack against the west side of Ponyri, but Soviet artillery delays the effort until 2100 hours.

3. 7 July, 1100 hours: 86.Infanterie-Division attacks and captures Hill 257.1 east of Ponyri.

4. 7 July, 1200 hours: a renewed attack by 292.Infanterie-Division fights its way into northern Ponyri, forcing Enshin to commit his reserves.

5. 7 July: 9.Panzer-Division attempts to outflank Ponyri by advancing towards Bityug; however, it takes all day to advance just 3km.

6. 7/8 July: elements of 3rd Tank Corps arrive to reinforce the defence of Ponyri; this enables local counterattacks, which regain some ground in Ponyri.

7. Afternoon, 8 July: 18.Panzer-Division attacks into Ponyri with only a single Panzergrenadier regiment, but is repulsed by artillery fire.

8. 8 July: 9.Panzer-Division attacks all day towards Ponyri-2, but resistance from Soviet tank and anti-tank units in the 'Box Woods' blocks any further progress. Soviet counterattacks force 9.Panzer-Division onto the defensive.

9. 0615 hours, 9 July: in one last attempt, 292.Infanterie-Division and part of 18.Panzer-Division mount a coordinated attack. They manage to surround the 1023rd Rifle Regiment in Ponyri.

10. 2200 hours, 9 July: a counterattack by 4th Guards Airborne Division links up with the trapped Soviet infantry inside Ponyri. Soon after this, the Germans shift to the defence in this sector.

THE BATTLE FOR PONYRI, 7–9 JULY 1943

Although Harpe's XXXXI Panzerkorps spends three days attempting to secure the small town of Ponyri, Soviet resistance cannot be overcome and only part of the town is captured. Efforts to outflank the Soviet defences fail.

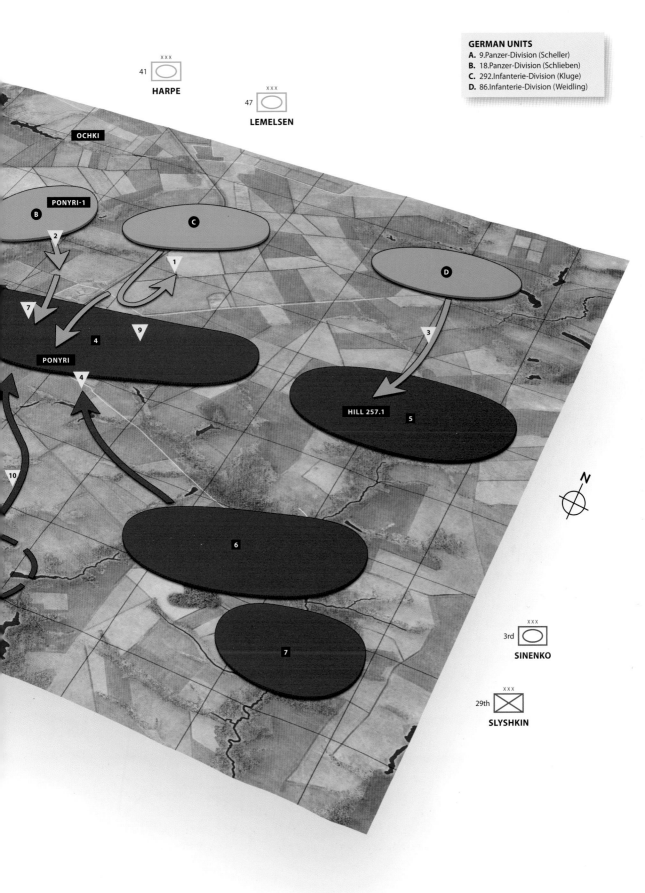

GERMAN UNITS
A. 9.Panzer-Division (Scheller)
B. 18.Panzer-Division (Schlieben)
C. 292.Infanterie-Division (Kluge)
D. 86.Infanterie-Division (Weidling)

41 XXX HARPE

47 XXX LEMELSEN

OCHKI

PONYRI-1

B

C

D

2

1

7

9

4

PONYRI

4

3

HILL 257.1

5

10

6

7

3rd XXX SINENKO

29th XXX SLYSHKIN

N

the infantry to hold it, so around noon he shifted his axis 5km eastwards, to attack Hill 257 north of Ol'khovatka. Such a lateral move across the front of an alert enemy was controversial, and Kampfgruppe Burmeister's decision to radically change the axis of attack was a poor tactical decision. The Soviets had two batteries of 85mm anti-aircraft guns to support 75th Guards Rifle Division's defence north of Ol'khovatka, and they were able to score long-range hits on Major Sauvant's Tigers, destroying one of them. T-34s from Grigor'ev's 16th Tank Corps supported the Soviet infantry positions from defilade positions. Hammered by Soviet anti-tank guns, anti-aircraft guns, artillery and dug-in Soviet tanks, Kampfgruppe Burmeister engaged in a protracted seven-hour battle with 70th Guards Rifle Division, and failed to capture Hill 257. Around 2100 hours Kampfgruppe Burmeister finally broke off the action and retreated 2km, having lost three more PzKpfw IV destroyed and many other tanks damaged. Although 2.Panzer-Division claimed to have knocked out ten more tanks, five anti-tank guns and twelve 85mm AA guns, it had failed to seize its designated objectives. The Germans did take some prisoners, including Leytenant Vasily T. Tkachov from 164th Tank Brigade, who revealed the scale of Soviet forces committed in this sector.

One mystery surrounding the tank battle on 7 July near Ol'khovatka concerns the role of Major Aleksei F. Sankovsky's SU-152 from 1541st Heavy Self-Propelled Artillery Regiment. Soviet sources claimed that Sankovsky's Su-152 single-handedly destroyed 10 Tigers and Ferdinands around Ol'khovatka on this day. It is possible that Sankovsky played a role in destroying the single Tiger and may have damaged others, but no Ferdinands were in this sector. Sankovsky's unit was apparently attached to 16th Tank Corps, but the records are unclear. Nevertheless, Sankovsky and his Su-152 were lionized as 'animal hunters' and other claims credited him with victories near Ponyri, also on 7 July. Thus, it appears that whatever role Sankovsky played during the battle of Kursk, the *Zvierboy* nickname was purely a propaganda invention intended to create the idea that the Red Army had a solution to the Tiger and Ferdinand.

Before Kessel's 20.Panzer-Division could make any progress westwards, Vasil'ev's 19th Tank Corps conducted a spoiling attack against 31.Infanterie-Division around 0800 hours. Kessel was forced to dispatch some of his panzers to repulse this armoured jab, which prevented him from launching his own attack until noon. When 20.Panzer-Division finally began advancing westwards toward the Snova River valley, Vasil'ev's tanks were blocking the way. A battalion-size tank action ensued south of Gnilets. Kessel's panzers claimed five enemy tanks knocked out, but then ran into a minefield and lost several of their own. Overall, 20.Panzer-Division gained very little ground and essentially served as a flank guard.

The third day of *Zitadelle* had been another frustrating one for AOK 9, since it had

At Ol'khovatka and Teploye, the Soviets dug in many of their tanks to increase survivability. In a concealed position like this, the Germans would have to get much closer to achieve a 'kill' with a hit on the turret. Note that this is an older T-34 Model 1942, many of which were still in use. (Author's collection)

failed to seriously dent Rokossovsky's second line at any point or even to gain any tactically useful ground. Everywhere, the Soviet defences had proven tough and resolute. Model was consuming manpower and ammunition and getting nowhere, which he knew was setting AOK 9 up for failure. On 7 July AOK 9 suffered another 2,861 casualties, including 657 dead or missing. Ammunition and fuel stockpiles were being consumed rapidly and Model made an urgent request to OKH for 100,000 rounds of anti-tank ammunition – a clear indication that the offensive had been run on a logistical shoestring.

The Luftwaffe was still doing well in the skies over the north front, but its level of air superiority was slipping; moreover, 16th Air Army was beginning to influence the ground fighting. On 7 July 1.Flieger-Division flew 1,687 sorties and lost 9 aircraft, while 16th Air Army flew 1,185 sorties and lost 43 aircraft. However, the Soviets could replace their air losses by transferring units from Bryansk's Front's unengaged 15th Air Army. The arrival of 234th Fighter Division restored Rudenko's fighter strength.

8 JULY

During the night of 7/8 July, Model committed Generalleutnant Dietrich von Saucken's 4.Panzer-Division and assigned it to Lemelsen's corps. He intended to make a major push with 2. and 4. Panzer divisions at first light to seize Teploye, which was near the boundary between the Soviet 13th and 70th armies, believing that a penetration here would create a substantial breach in Rokossovsky's second line of defence. Model now had five of his panzer divisions committed to battle, while his infantry divisions were only tasked with defending the flanks.

As a preliminary move, Saucken's 4.Panzer-Division supported an attack by 20.Panzer-Division at 0515 hours to clear out Samodurovka, which took about an hour. However, Lemelsen's corps allowed part of the morning to pass by and did not begin a serious push until late morning. At that point, 4.Panzer-Division advanced towards Teploye, which was defended by General-Major Aleksandr I. Kiselev's 140th Siberian Rifle Division. Kiselev was an NKVD officer with very little frontline experience; many of his troops also lacked this, being NKVD guards from prison camps in the Gulag. Normally such troops would have been easy meat for an experienced German unit like 4. Panzer-Division, but Kiselev's division was amply supported by 3rd Anti-Tank Brigade and 79th Tank Brigade, which had dug in its tanks. Saucken attacked with about 50 tanks, including Major Sauvant's last three operational Tigers, and was able to overrun part of Teploye. One of Kiselev's battalions – 2nd Battalion/96th Rifle Regiment – was demolished in the village, but Saucken ran into trouble just south

Soviet forward observers bring the fire of 4th Artillery Corps down on the German spearheads. Soviet artillery support was a powerful factor in the success of the Soviet defence, and it would be increasingly important in unlocking German defensive positions in the counter-offensive that followed *Zitadelle*. (From the fonds of the RGAKFD in Krasnogorsk via Stavka)

HIGH-WATER MARK AT TEPLOYE, 1300 HOURS, 8 JULY 1943 (PP. 64–65)

By the fourth day of *Zitadelle* Model had committed all his armour, including 4.Panzer-Division. With this influx of fresh men and materiel, Model hoped to capture the heights around the village of Teploye and put a major dent in Rokossovsky's second line of defence. After skirmishing on the northern outskirts of Teploye on the morning of 8 July, 4.Panzer-Division mounted an all-out attack with Kampfgruppe Burmeister (I./Panzer-Regiment 35), supported by the last three operational Tigers from schwere Panzer-Abteilung 505, panzergrenadiers, artillery and Stukas. Normally, this type of German combined-arms attack would have sliced through the Soviet defences, but here the Germans met their match. The Soviet defenders at Teploye, consisting of 140th Rifle Division and 3rd Anti-Tank Brigade, were heavily entrenched behind deep minefields and well supported by artillery. T-34s from 79th Tank Brigade were dug in and only visible at close range.

Here a platoon of PzKpfw IVs from Panzer-Regiment 35 (**1**) and a single Tiger (**2**) are attempting to seize a Soviet-held hill that is defended by dug-in tanks and anti-tank guns (**3**). Despite rolling Stuka attacks, the Soviet defence remains unbroken; three Pz IV tanks are totally destroyed and many other German tanks are damaged. The Soviets lose at least four T-34s (**4**) and one KV-1 (**5**) in this action, plus a number of anti-tank guns (**6**).

As with post-war exaggerations about tank combat at Prokhorovka on the southern side of the Kursk salient, the scale of tank battles around Ponyri, Ol'khovatka and Teploye has often been depicted as simultaneously involving hundreds of tanks on both sides. In fact, most of the tank battles were battalion- and regimental-size actions. In any event, the failure of the heavily reinforced 4.Panzer-Division at Teploye symbolized the high-water mark of Model's forces.

of Teploye, when he encountered mines and intense anti-tank fire. Following the tradition of leading from the front, Saucken moved his command vehicle into Teploye, but got stuck when a wooden bridge he tried to cross collapsed. For two crucial hours he was pre-occupied with extracting himself, leaving his operations officer, Major Hans Lutz, to run the attack. When the German tanks came under direct fire, they stopped advancing and engaged in a protracted gunnery duel with the Soviet tanks and anti-tank guns. The German panzers tried to use their advantage in long-range gunnery, but the dug-in Soviet tanks proved extremely difficult to hit. Despite firing for hours, losses were low on both sides. 4.Panzer-Division had many vehicles hit but only 3 PzKpfw IV destroyed, and its personnel losses were just 74 troops killed and 210 wounded. Soviet losses were estimated at 4 T-34s and 1 KV-1 knocked out, 20 anti-tank guns destroyed and 200–300 troops killed.

On Saucken's left flank, Kampfgruppe Burmeister from 2.Panzer-Division made an attack southwards against Hill 274, which was defended by Polkovnik Ivan A. Gusev's 70th Guards Rifle Division and a medley of armour units from 16th Tank Corps. Like Saucken's division, Burmeister attacked relatively late and ran into a wall of mines and anti-tank fire. Another protracted gunnery duel ensued, and Burmeister eventually broke off the action when his vehicles ran low on fuel and ammunition. The rest of 2.Panzer-Division mounted a weak attack against Soviet defences north of Ol'khovatka, but only gained a small amount of ground. Although Lemelsen's armour never really came close to breaking through, Rokossovsky was concerned enough to order 11th Guards Tank Brigade to be positioned right at the inter-army boundary near Hill 274. This unit launched a strong armoured spoiling attack around 1700 hours that threatened Burmeister's exposed flank. Unable to take his objective, Burmeister pulled back to his starting positions. Although Gusev's 70th Guards Rifle Division had suffered considerable losses, it could still hold its positions.

While Lemelsen grappled with Soviet armour around Teploye and Ol'khovatka, Harpe tried to clinch a tactical victory at Ponyri. Allowing the exhausted 292.Infanterie-Division to rest, Harpe sent in Schlieben's 18.Panzer-Division to clear the town out street by street. Soviet mines and artillery knocked out four Ferdinands, but Schlieben's troops were able to secure the train station and the central part of the town by evening. Although Enshin's 307th Rifle Division suffered heavy losses, his artillery support was intact, and Pukhov was bringing up the fresh 4th Guards Airborne Division. Enshin counterattacked toward Ponyri's train station with the remnants of his infantry and some tanks from the newly arrived 51st Tank Brigade. While AOK 9 had few reserves left, Rokossovsky still had plenty of units ready to commit to battle as needed, which made Soviet reserves seem inexhaustible to the Germans. By day's end Ponyri was wrecked from one end to another, but the Germans still held only half the town.

An American-built A-20 bomber operated by 16th Air Army's 221st Bomber Aviation Division. The Soviet VVS (Military Air Forces) used this Lend-Lease aircraft in the ground-attack role and it enjoyed success against Kampfgruppe Burmeister of 2.Panzer-Division. (Author's collection)

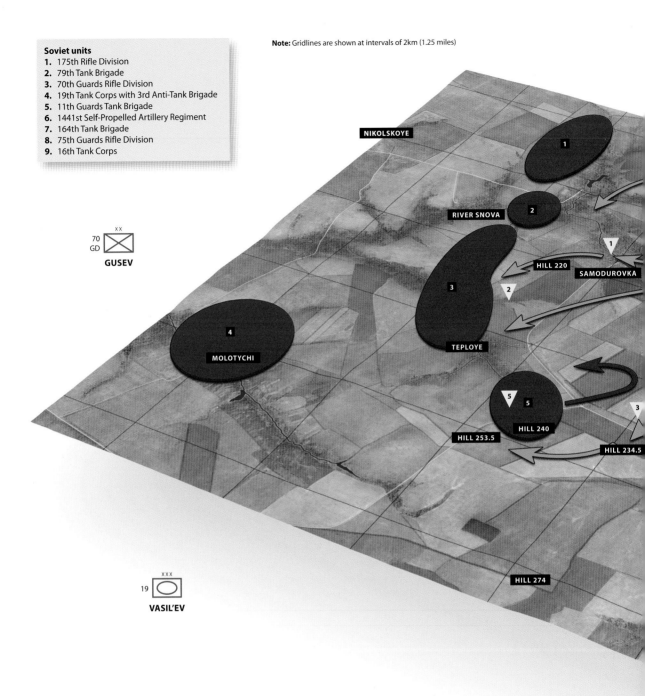

Note: Gridlines are shown at intervals of 2km (1.25 miles)

Soviet units
1. 175th Rifle Division
2. 79th Tank Brigade
3. 70th Guards Rifle Division
4. 19th Tank Corps with 3rd Anti-Tank Brigade
5. 11th Guards Tank Brigade
6. 1441st Self-Propelled Artillery Regiment
7. 164th Tank Brigade
8. 75th Guards Rifle Division
9. 16th Tank Corps

NIKOLSKOYE

RIVER SNOVA

70 GD — GUSEV

HILL 220

SAMODUROVKA

TEPLOYE

MOLOTYCHI

HILL 240

HILL 253.5

HILL 234.5

HILL 274

19 — VASIL'EV

▼ EVENTS

1. 0515–0615 hours, 8 July: the newly arrived 4.Panzer-Division supports an attack by 20.Panzer-Division that secures Samodurovka, thereby protecting XXXXVII Panzerkorps' right flank.

2. 1300 hours, 8 July: the entire 4.Panzer-Division, along with three Tiger tanks, attacks 70th Guards Rifle Division positions around Teploye. The attack is halted by intense fire from anti-tank guns and dug-in tanks from 19th Tank Corps.

3. Afternoon, 8 July: Kampfgruppe Burmeister from 2.Panzer-Division attempts to advance towards Hill 274, but is halted near Hill 240.

4. 8 July: the rest of 2.Panzer-Division advances towards Hill 257 and the northern approaches to Ol'khovatka, but makes only limited progress.

5. 1700 hours, 8 July: 19th Tank Corps counterattacks near Hill 240 with 11th Guards Tank Brigade. Although the counterattack fails, XXXXVII Panzerkorps has too few infantry to hold its limited gains, and pulls back into defensive positions.

THE BATTLE FOR TEPLOYE AND OL'KHOVATKA, 8 JULY 1943

Lemelsen's XXXXVII Panzerkorps attempts to break through Rokossovsky's second line of defence, but fails. This is the high-water mark of *Zitadelle* for AOK 9.

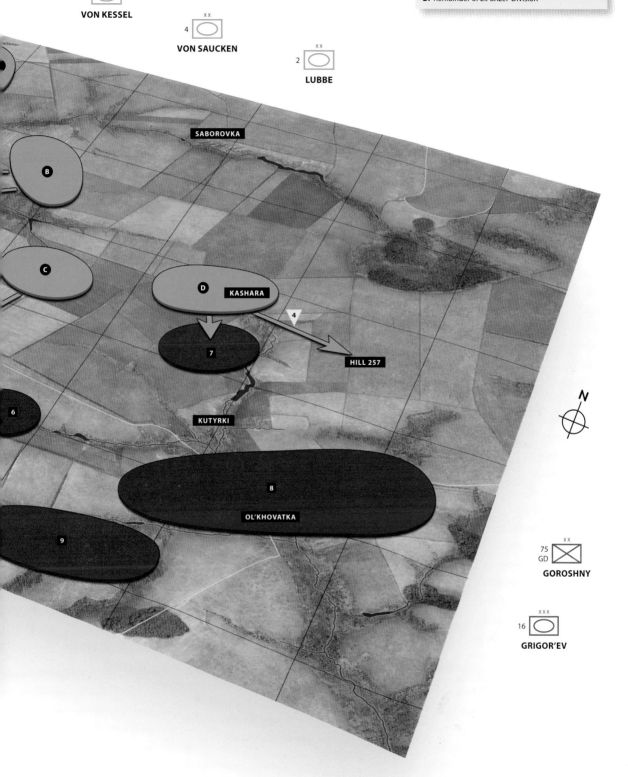

GERMAN UNITS
A. 20.Panzer-Division
B. 4.Panzer-Division
C. Kampfgruppe Burmeister, 2.Panzer-Division
D. Remainder of 2.Panzer-Division

20 — VON KESSEL

4 — VON SAUCKEN

2 — LUBBE

SABOROVKA

B

C

D — KASHARA

4

7

HILL 257

6

KUTYRKI

8

OL'KHOVATKA

9

75 GD — GOROSHNY

16 — GRIGOR'EV

N

69

On 8 July AOK 9 suffered another 3,220 casualties, including 764 dead or missing, but had little to show for these losses. Despite afternoon rain showers, 1.Flieger-Division managed to fly 1,173 sorties, against 913 sorties flown by 16th Air Army. The Luftwaffe was still inflicting disproportionate losses upon the Soviet flyers – losing 2 aircraft destroyed and 9 damaged for 49 destroyed and 11 damaged – but fuel shortages were starting to curtail operations. By the end of the fourth day of *Zitadelle*, Model knew that most of his Tigers and Ferdinands were out of action, that his infantry strength was nearly expended and that his air support could not operate at this tempo for much longer. Nevertheless, he decided to regroup his forces during the night and try for one last big push, hoping to force a breakthrough.

9 JULY

Rudenko's 16th Air Army started the day by making a mass attack at dawn with 110 Pe-2s and 62 Il-2s against Lemelsen's XXXXVII Panzerkorps. The German fighter cover was slow in responding to this scale of effort, and the German panzer divisions began their day under strafing and bombing attack. Over the course of the day 1.Flieger-Division was able to knock down 20 Soviet aircraft, but lost 8 of its own with 2 more damaged.

Lemelsen intended to launch an all-out attack with 2., 4. and 20. Panzer divisions, supported by Stukas, but it simply did not materialize. 2.Panzer-Division kept its panzers in reserve and only committed its panzergrenadiers against Grigor'ev's 16th Tank Corps, which had positioned itself north of Ol'khovatka; however, nothing was achieved and the Germans broke off the attack. Likewise, 4.Panzer-Division found itself facing Vasil'ev's 19th Tank Corps at Teploye, and opted to postpone its attack for at least 24 hours. Major Sauvant's Tiger battalion was pulled back to repair its battle-worn vehicles. 20.Panzer-Division screened the corps' right flank and quietly shifted to the defensive. Throughout the day, the Soviets mounted small-scale counterattacks against Lemelsen's corps, but the situation in the Teploye–Ol'khovatka sector essentially devolved into a mutual stand-off, with no major offensive action by either side.

Harpe was more active with his XXXXI Panzerkorps in the Ponyri sector. At 0615 hours he launched a concentric attack against Enshin's positions in southern Ponyri with both 292.Infanterie-Division and 18.Panzer-Division, supported by all available artillery. Enshin's 1023rd Rifle Regiment held its ground, but was gradually encircled during the course of the day. The Soviet 3rd Tank Corps committed some armour to assist his defence, but lost eight tanks around Ponyri. As Enshin's situation grew more desperate, Pukhov decided to commit 4th Guards Airborne Division to counterattack into

A knocked-out PzKpfw IV medium tank belonging to 2. Panzer-Division's Panzer-Regiment 3. Kampfgruppe Burmeister lost eight PzKpfw IVs on 7 July: five to air attack, and three to direct fire north of Ol'khovatka. The tank losses suffered by AOK 9 during *Zitadelle* were never crippling, but many more vehicles were rendered inoperative by a combination of battle damage and mechanical failure. (Author's collection)

Ponyri. After several hours of desperate fighting, the paratroopers were able to link up with Enshin's isolated troops by about 2200 hours. Another day of heavy attritional combat around Ponyri had led to no real change in the tactical situation, but now the German divisions engaged were exhausted. German efforts to outflank Ponyri with 9.Panzer-Division and 86.Infanterie-Division met with a similar lack of success. Overall, AOK 9 suffered another 1,861 casualties, including 456 dead or missing.

A Sturmpanzer that has been destroyed by a direct hit from a large projectile. Sturmpanzer-Abteilung 216 lost one-quarter of its vehicles during *Zitadelle*, but continued to play a role in the fighting around Orel. (Author's collection)

10 JULY

Lemelsen's XXXXVII Panzerkorps finally mounted its multi-division attack around 0700 hours with all three panzer divisions, assisted by most of 1.Flieger-Division's ground support aircraft. A mixed Soviet force, with tanks and infantry, offered stiff resistance, but a two-pronged attack by 2. and 4. Panzer divisions was finally able to clear Teploye by 1800 hours. It had taken most of a day for two complete German panzer divisions to seize a single, small town – a rather hollow tactical victory. Lemelsen also directed 2.Panzer-Division to improve its position north of Ol'khovatka, but it was unable to make progress.

Model decided to commit Generalleutnant August Schmidt's 10. Panzergrenadier Division to relieve 292.Infanterie-Division at Ponyri, but he wanted Harpe to make one more push with his remaining troops and armour. The new German assault caught 4th Guards Airborne Division before it could consolidate its position and managed to push them back a little, but then the same old see-saw fighting around Ponyri train station dragged on for most of the day. 3rd Tank Corps continued to feed small amounts of armour into the town to support the infantry, and four more T-34s were destroyed. Rudenko's 16th Air Army launched another series of massed attacks with 106 Pe-2s, 65 DB-7s and 37 Il-2s against German troop concentrations north of Ponyri. Artillery barrages from both sides blasted the town into burning wreckage and cratered the surrounding landscape. By evening, the Germans controlled about two-thirds

Two disabled Ferdinands from schwere Panzerjäger-Abteilung 654 left abandoned near Ponyri after *Zitadelle* ended. These Ferdinands were disabled by mines. The Germans had great difficulty recovering these 65-ton vehicles from the battlefield under fire – resulting in a significant number being abandoned. (Author's collection)

The situation at the end of *Zitadelle*, 10 July 1943.

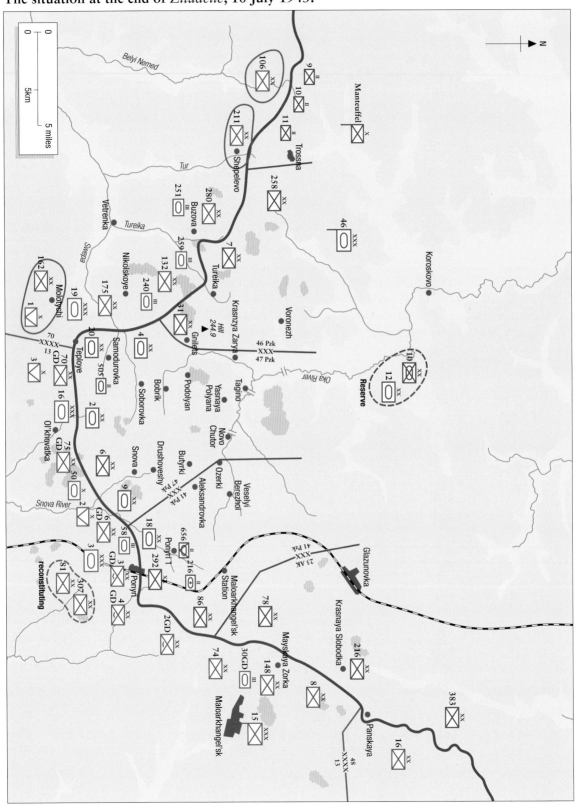

of Ponyri, but the Soviets still held the southern part of the town. Pukhov finally pulled Enshin's 307th Rifle Division out of Ponyri and turned the defence of the town over to 3rd and 4th Guards Airborne divisions. Schmidt's division also arrived to replace 292.Infanterie-Division during the night and Harpe's corps began transitioning to the defence. Overall, AOK 9 suffered another 2,560 casualties, including 564 dead or missing.

Despite Rudenko's success in getting his close air support groups into action, 1.Flieger-Division's fighters still maintained effective air superiority over most of the northern sector and inflicted painful losses on the 16th Air Army. On 10 July 1.Flieger-Division lost 7 aircraft but managed to destroy 43 Soviet fighters. The failure of General-Major Andrei Yumashev's 6th Fighter Corps to achieve air superiority did not go unnoticed, and he was relieved of command.

Model could clearly see that his AOK 9 had reached the end of its ability to either gain significant terrain objectives or destroy Rokossovsky's reserves. Therefore, there was little point in AOK 9 continuing its role in *Zitadelle*, and he ordered all his forces to transition to the defence. OKH was not happy to hear that Model was breaking off his offensive while Manstein's offensive with Heeresgruppe Süd was still making progress against Nikolai Vatutin's Voronezh Front. Although OKH made suggestions that AOK 9 could shift its attack axis westward into the XXXXVI Panzerkorps sector to catch Rokossovsky off guard, Model simply ignored these. He knew that a major Soviet counter-offensive against the Orel salient would not be long in coming, and wanted to rest his forces prior to this next test of strength.

11 JULY

This was a relatively quiet day on the northern front, with both AOK 9 and Central Front trying to reconstitute their battered frontline units. The only offensive action was a local one by the Soviets to recover some of the high ground lost north of Ol'khovatka. However, both sides used their artillery to pound the frontline units and air attacks to target units behind the frontline. Even with every division shifted to the defence and no major Soviet attacks, Model's AOK 9 still suffered another 1,480 casualties, including 304 dead or missing – a clear indicator of the dominant role of artillery in the battle.

In order to cover the shift to the defence on the ground, 1.Flieger-Division flew 933 sorties and maintained air superiority over the northern sector, while 16th Air Army flew only 301 sorties. The Luftwaffe used its air superiority to attack concentrations of Soviet artillery and armour, to take pressure off Model's ground troops. As *Zitadelle* ended on the northern sector, it was clear that 1.Flieger-Division had won the air battle against 16th Air Army between 5 and 11 July – a fact that Soviet-era histories would later conceal. While Luftflotte 6 lost 57 aircraft destroyed in action and another 60 from other causes during *Zitadelle*, 16th Air Army lost 439 aircraft. Although German fighter units had completely outfought their opponents over a week of sustained combat, the Soviet ground attack units had bravely fought through the German fighter cover to accomplish their missions.

In contrast, the situation in the ground fighting was dismal for AOK 9. Between 5 and 11 July AOK 9 had barely advanced 15km at the deepest point, yet it had suffered a total of 22,201 casualties, including 4,691 dead or missing. This was the highest total loss rate for any German Army in a one-week period since Operation *Barbarossa* began two years prior, including AOK 6's losses in Stalingrad in September and October 1942. Four of the infantry divisions involved in the offensive – 78., 86., 258. and 292. – had suffered crippling losses totalling between 35 and 57 per-cent of their infantry strength. It is particularly surprising that the units in the supporting XXIII Armeekorps and XXXXVI Panzerkorps suffered almost as badly as the divisions involved in the *schwerpunkt*. The equipment losses from XXXXVI Panzerkorps' three infantry divisions used in *Zitadelle* (7., 31. and 258.) totalled only one 10.5cm l.FH18 howitzer, nineteen 3.7cm Pak and five 5cm Pak, but their infantry battalions had been shredded, with average strengths reduced from 400–450 to 185–280 in less than a week of combat.

On the other hand, losses of German armoured vehicles were relatively modest. The six panzer divisions involved in AOK 9's part of *Zitadelle* lost a total of only 29 tanks destroyed, including 3 Tigers from schwere Panzer-Abteilung 505. In addition, schwere Panzerjäger-Regiment 656 lost 19 Ferdinands and 6 Sturmpanzers. The seven Sturmgeschütz-Abteilung supporting AOK 9 lost 17 StuGs destroyed and another 61 damaged; 63 per-cent of its tanks were still combat ready when the offensive was called off. Altogether, AOK 9 lost 71 tanks, tank destroyers and assault guns destroyed during *Zitadelle* – or less than 10 per-cent of its original armoured force. Another 308 armoured fighting vehicles were damaged and under repair, but 75 per-cent would return to service within two weeks. Even before the dust had settled, Soviet sources made extravagant claims that over 200 German tanks had been destroyed on the northern front on the first day of *Zitadelle* and 400 of them overall, including an incredible claim that in one 20-minute attack a group of Il-2 Sturmoviks destroyed 70 tanks from 9.Panzer-Division. To buttress these claims, Soviet historians created the myth that a huge, four-day tank battle involving up to 1,000 tanks on each side had occurred between Ponyri and Ol'khovatka – the truth was that most of the tank engagements were small-scale company- or battalion-size actions. On the northern front there was no great clash of armour, just a series of skirmishes. Consequently, when *Zitadelle* ended Model was left with almost 500 tanks, tank destroyers and assault guns still operational.

Rokossovsky's Central Front suffered heavy casualties during *Zitadelle*, although the exact figures are hard to pin down. Soviet-era statistics claim that Central Front suffered a total of 33,897 casualties, including 15,336 dead or missing, during the defensive phase of the battle of Kursk. However, German sources claim that Soviet losses were probably much higher. This is not unreasonable, given that Rokossovsky's forces were unable to contribute much to the opening phase of the ensuing Operation *Kutusov*. It is clear that 15th, 81st and 307th Rifle divisions were crippled in the fighting and that several other rifle divisions suffered heavily as well. Soviet losses of armour were heavier than German ones, but the scale is not well documented. Rodin's 2nd Tank Army lost 138 tanks destroyed and 80 more damaged during *Zitadelle*, representing 46 per-cent of their starting strength. Pukhov's 13th Army committed all of its 270 tanks to battle and probably lost 30 per-cent of them – roughly 80 tanks. Thus, Rokossovsky's Central Front most likely lost over 200 tanks destroyed and between 100 and 200 damaged during *Zitadelle*. The Germans also made some extravagant claims about Soviet tank losses, but it appears that they achieved no better than a 2.8:1 'kill ratio', which was not enough to justify the sacrifices made in *Zitadelle*. Both sides failed to incapacitate each other's main armoured reserves.

OPERATION *KUTUSOV*: THE SOVIET COUNTER-OFFENSIVE, 12 JULY–18 AUGUST

While *Zitadelle* was going on in the AOK 9 sector, 2.Panzerarmee was on a high state of alert, looking for any indicators of offensive activity by the Soviet Western or Bryansk fronts. Although there was little happening apart from the usual local ground skirmishing, Soviet artillery regularly harassed 2.Panzerarmee, which suffered over 1,000 casualties in the first ten days of July. However, once it became clear that Model had suspended his offensive, the situation rapidly changed. Stavka wanted to begin Operation *Kutusov* immediately, before Model had a chance to re-deploy any of his panzer divisions to support 2.Panzerarmee. On 11 July reconnaissance units from both the Western and Bryansk fronts began probing aggressively in strengths of up to battalion size, all along the front of 2.Panzerarmee, in order to pinpoint German minefields and defensive strongpoints.

Although 2.Panzerarmee had well-prepared defences and had 5.Panzer-Division in tactical reserve, its command and control was disrupted at this moment by the relief and arrest of its commander, General der Infanterie Erich-Heinrich Clößner, by the Gestapo. Heeresgruppe Mitte had indeed become a breeding ground for the anti-Nazi resistance, with Kluge and his operations officer Oberst Henning von Tresckow at the centre of the conspiracy. However, Clößner was simply guilty of shooting his mouth off at the wrong time. In any case, his removal left 2.Panzerarmee without firm leadership at a key moment. Recognizing the danger posed by Clößner's fate, Model immediately asked OKH that he be given dual command over both AOK 9 and 2.Panzerarmee. OKH, however, did not grant this. Consequently, a number of German senior leaders saw the Soviet counter-offensive shaping up, but their responses were uncoordinated. Rendulic, in command of XXXV Armeekorps, was the most responsive; he was able to identify the most likely sector where Bryansk Front was going to attack and re-deployed his best anti-tank units to reinforce the threatened area. However, General der Infanterie Friedrich Gollwitzer's LIII Armeekorps took no special measures, trusting that its defences would hold until the panzers arrived.

Soviet artillery fire during the opening stages of Operation *Kutusov*. 2.Panzerarmee was hit by a mass of men and materiel that quickly threatened the German hold on the Orel salient. (Author's collection)

The Bryansk Front offensive, 12–21 July 1943.

1. 0605 hours, 12 July: six rifle divisions from Bryansk Front's 3rd and 63rd armies attack the boundary between the German 56. and 262. Infantry divisions. However, Rendulic's XXXV Armeekorps is well prepared for the assault, and inflicts heavy losses on the supporting Soviet armour.
2. Noon, 13 July: the Soviet 3rd Army commits its 1st Guards Tank Corps, which enables Bryansk Front to make small gains. Rendulic commits his corps reserve, 36.Infanterie-Division.
3. Late on 13 July: AOK 9 sends 2. and 8. Panzer divisions forwards to prevent a Soviet breakthrough.
4. 14–16 July: due to the commitment of the second echelon 25th Rifle Corps, 3rd Army is able to push back Rendulic's infantry after three days of hard fighting. However, the arrival of the two panzer divisions halts the Soviet advance.
5. 18 July: 63rd Army commits seven rifle divisions against the right flank of XXXV Armeekorps, eventually forcing Rendulic to pull back.
6. 1030 hours, 19 July: Rybalko's 3rd Guards Tank Army enters the battle and forces both panzer divisions to cede ground. Rybalko's armour is ordered to push towards Otrada.
7. 20 July: 12.Panzer-Division arrives in Orel to defend the eastern approaches against Rybalko's armour.
8. 0300 hours, 21 July: Bryansk Front decides to split 3rd Guards Tank Army, sending two corps towards Otrada and diverting 12th Tank Corps to overrun 262.Infanterie-Division. The attack succeeds, but Rybalko's armour is split on two divergent axes of advance.

German frontline morning, 12 July
Soviet frontline evening, 13 July
Soviet frontline evening, 16 July
German frontline evening, 21 July

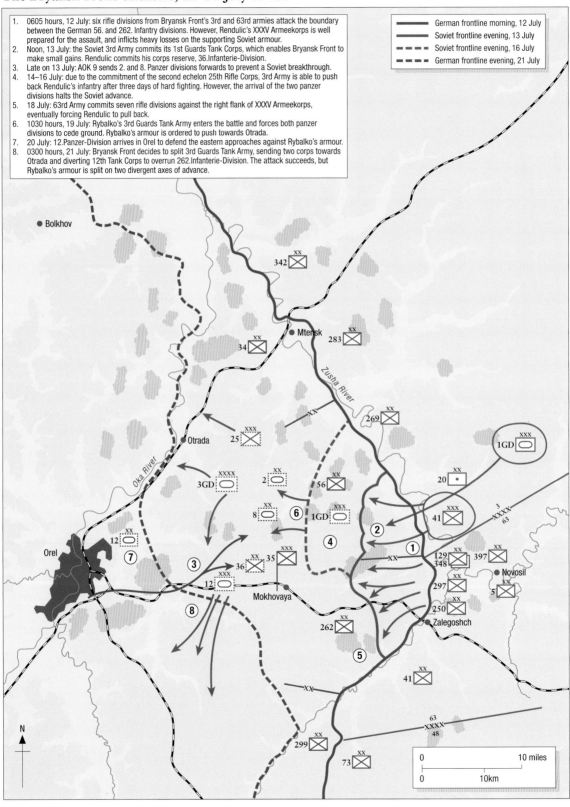

12 JULY

At 0330 hours Operation *Kutusov* began with the Western and Bryansk fronts starting a massive artillery barrage against the left and right flanks of 2.Panzerarmee. Stavka had provided these two fronts with an unprecedented amount of artillery – three breakthrough artillery corps and two separate artillery divisions – in order to flatten the German defences. German troops on the Eastern Front had never been on the receiving end of so much concentrated firepower. On both fronts, the artillery preparation lasted two and a half hours and inflicted great damage on the German frontline positions.

Stavka intended that General-polkovnik Markian M. Popov's Bryansk Front would provide the main effort in Operation *Kutusov*, using 3rd and 63rd armies to overwhelm Rendulic's XXXV Armeekorps at the face of the Orel salient, while General Vasily D. Sokolovsky's Western Front used 11th Guards Army to attack the flank in the LIII Armeekorps sector. Model believed that Popov's Bryansk Front was the main threat and that Sokolovsky would only mount diversionary attacks.

Popov's main striking power was concentrated at the boundary between the German 56. and 262. Infantry divisions, west of Novosil. General-Leytenant Aleksandr V. Gorbatov's 3rd Army attacked the right flank of 56.Infanterie-Division with three divisions from his 41st Rifle Corps at 0605 hours, while General-Leytenant Vladimir Ia. Kolpakchi's 63rd Army attacked the left flank of 262.Infanterie-Division with four rifle divisions. Kolpakchi's was the main effort, supported by 2nd Breakthrough Artillery Corps and General-Leytenant Nikolai F. Naumenko's 15th Air Army. Despite the weight of fire directed at Rendulic's troops, the German defence was not broken and the Soviet infantry carved a mere 5km advance into the German outer defensive belt. Popov exercised very poor control over the battle and allowed 3rd and 63rd armies to essentially fight their own actions.

Ritter von Greim reacted immediately to Popov's offensive, and based upon Model's assessment committed all of Luftflotte 6 against 15th Air Army. Naumenko's pilots were significantly less experienced than those of Rudenko's 16th Air Army, and stood little chance against 1.Flieger-Division, which inflicted 6:1 losses upon them. After losing more than 50 aircraft, 15th Air Army failed to gain control of the air over its sector, and Bryansk Front consequently did not receive the intended close air support. Popov's attack was halted, suffering heavy losses. Rendulic requested reinforcements to further strengthen his defence.

Although the German defence achieved a temporary tactical victory against Popov's front, Gollwitzer's LIII Armeekorps was caught by surprise by the scale of Sokolovsky's offensive. Bagramyan's 11th Guards Army massed six divisions from its 8th and 16th Guards Rifle corps and 8th Breakthrough Artillery Corps against the boundary between 211. and 293. Infantry divisions. Generalmajor Karl Arndt's 293.Infanterie-Division occupied excellent defensive positions on high ground south of the Zhizdra River, but the weight of Russian artillery succeeded in smashing his division's left flank in a matter of hours, before the Germans could react. Due to the commitment of all of Luftflotte 6 against Bryansk Front's attack sector, General-Leytenant Mikhail M. Gromov's 1st Air Army was able to gain complete air superiority over the Ulyanovo sector. Bagramyan's rifle divisions

Infantry from Bryansk Front cautiously moving forward as the artillery barrage subsides. Bryansk Front's attack was neither well planned nor well directed, leading to extremely heavy losses. (Author's collection)

surged forward onto the high ground, with several Guards Tank brigades in support. Gollwitzer immediately requested that Generalmajor Ernst Fäckenstedt's 5.Panzer-Division, which was equipped with 100 tanks and was in reserve positions 30km to the south-west, should move up to prevent a Soviet breakthrough. Fäckenstedt was a career staff officer with no previous command experience – not the sort of officer who should have been leading a panzer division – and his employment of the tactical reserve was faulty. Instead of 'marching to the sound of the guns' at Ulyanovo, where Gollwitzer's front was collapsing, he opted to move into 211.Infanterie-Division's sector, where the front was still holding. This safe, textbook manoeuvre allowed Fäckenstedt to organize his dispersed division before heading into battle, but it delayed the German response. Unchecked, Bagramyan's vanguard units advanced 10km on the first day and reached Ulyanovo. Over the next two weeks Fäckenstedt's poorly handled division would lose 55 of its tanks – more than any other German panzer division involved in the campaign.

Despite Bagramyan's success, the Germans were more concerned about Bryansk Front. The collapse of Arndt's 293.Infanterie-Division was worrisome, but it occurred in a remote, heavily wooded sector that was far from any significant objectives. OKH believed that Fäckenstedt's 5.Panzer-Division could seal off Bagramyan's penetration and devoted its main attention to stopping Popov. Many of the damaged Ferdinands had been repaired, and both schwere Panzerjäger-Abteilung 653 and 654, with 60 Ferdinands, were sent to reinforce Rendulic. Heeresgruppe Mitte's Kluge decided to transfer 8.Panzer-Division by rail from Vitebsk to reinforce the Orel salient, and the lead elements had already reached Orel. In order to replace 1.Flieger-Division's losses from *Zitadelle* and enable it to handle three Soviet air armies, the Luftwaffe pulled fighters from Heeresgruppe Nord's sector. Greim believed that the best way to shut down *Kutusov* was to deprive the Soviets of their air support, and he intended to use all available aircraft to smash Naumenko's 15th Air Army.

13 JULY

At first light, Greim committed eight Jagdgruppen over the eastern part of the Orel salient and caught 15th Air Army by surprise. Although Jagdgeschwader 51 had lost a number of veteran pilots during *Zitadelle*, it remained effective. Its pilots massacred Naumenko's close air support, shooting down fifty Il-2 Sturmoviks. During the course of the day 15th Air Army lost 44 more aircraft and was rendered combat ineffective. Luftflotte 6 lost 20 aircraft, including nine Fw-190s, but succeeded in depriving Popov of his air support.

Gorbatov's 3rd Army and Kolpachki's 63rd Army attacked again and committed their supporting tank regiments and brigades in order to create a breakthrough. However, Rendulic had positioned his best anti-tank units, including a company of the new Hornisse tank destroyers equipped with 8.8cm guns, in their path. Three regiments of KV-1S tanks attempted to break through the left flank of 262.Infanterie-Division. However, they ran into uncleared minefields and were shot to pieces by German panzerjägers; this battle proved to be the swan song for the KV-1 heavy tank. Rudenko's 16th Air Army transferred some of its Pe-2 bombers to support Popov's front, but the Soviet ground attacks failed to achieve a breakthrough. Nevertheless, Popov committed General-Major Mikhail F. Panov's 1st Guards Tank Corps to reinforce 3rd Army's attack. Rendulic promptly committed his reserve, Generalleutnant Hans Gollnick's 36.Infanterie-Division (mot.), to reinforce the area where the two Soviet armies were attacking; the arrival of the two Ferdinand battalions greatly increased his anti-tank capability. By evening, although the two Soviet armies had advanced between 9 and 12km, powerful German reinforcements were helping to stabilize the front.

General-Leytenant Pavel Belov's 61st Army joined in Bryansk Front's offensive by launching a supporting attack with three divisions of 9th Guards Rifle Corps against 208.Infanterie-Division east of Bolkhov. Surprisingly, this attack managed to cross the Oka River and create a small salient. 112. Infanterie-Division was able to assist in sealing off the breach, but this action left a Soviet bridgehead just 12km east of Bolkhov. Generalmajor Erpo Freiherr von Bodenhausen's 12.Panzer-Division, which had been in reserve around Orel throughout *Zitadelle*, was ordered to deal with Belov's breakthrough.

While the Luftwaffe played a major role in stopping Popov's Bryansk Front, it lacked the resources to be everywhere. As a result, Gromov's 1st Air Army was unopposed over the Ulyanovo sector. With this crucial air support, Bagramyan's 11th Guards Army succeeded in crushing the last defences of Arndt's 293.Infanterie-Division, and achieved a tactical breakthrough at Ulyanovo. Once it was clear that Arndt's line had been broken, Sokolovsky committed General-Major Vasily V. Butkov's 1st Tank Corps and General-Major Mikhail G. Sakhno's 5th Tank Corps to exploit the breakthrough. Fäckenstedt's 5.Panzer-Division and 211.Infanterie-Division managed to seal off the western side of the Soviet penetration by counterattacking 16th Guards Rifle Corps on Bagramyan's right flank, but the Soviet armour created a huge gap in 2.Panzerarmee's front. The only thing slowing Bagramyan's armour was the rough terrain and poor-quality roads in this remote sector. Although he still lacked authority over this sector, Model dispatched 12., 18. and 20. Panzer divisions to help counter Bagramyan's breakthrough. After two days of fighting, 2. Panzerarmee had suffered over 6,300 casualties.

German infantry in hasty fighting positions await the Soviet onslaught. No solid German defensive line had been broken during good weather before, but 2. Panzerarmee was forced to defend too much front with too few men. Despite armoured support, the Soviet counter-offensive rapidly ground up the frontline German infantry units. (Author's collection)

BAGRAMYAN'S BREAKTHROUGH, 0700 HOURS, 13 JULY 1943 (PP. 80–81)

Soviet Western Front began its counter-offensive, Operation *Kutusov*, at 0300 hours on 12 July 1943. General-polkovnik Ivan Bagramyan's 11th Guards Army attacked the northern side of the German defences in the Orel salient, held by LIII Armeekorps. On the first day of fighting, the Soviet guards rifle divisions burst through the German first line of defence, held by 211. and 293. Infantry divisions. Despite the arrival of 5.Panzer-Division, the German front could not be restored. On the second day of *Kutusov*, Bagramyan committed his armoured exploitation force – 1st and 5th Tank corps – and it smashed through the German second line of defence. By evening, Soviet armour had broken through the German infantry defences and penetrated deep into the flank of 2.Panzerarmee. However, Model was a master at shuffling his panzer reserves around, and he managed to prevent

Bagramyan from achieving a complete breakthrough. This was also the first time that the Soviets managed to break through a German defensive line in clear weather, despite the fact that the Germans had panzer and Luftwaffe support – a portent of the growing disparity between the two armies.

Here, Soviet tanks from 5th Tank Corps (**1**) and troops from 11th Guards Rifle Division (**2**) are overrunning the left wing of the German 293.Infanterie-Division's defence near Ulyanovo. A German infantry kampfgruppe (**3**) is unable to stop the torrent of T-34s (**4**) and infantry (**5**) smashing through its main line of resistance. A lone German Pak 38 (**6**) engages the T-34s in a one-sided action. Although Soviet casualties are heavy, 293.Infanterie-Division's line is broken.

14 JULY

During the afternoon, elements of 1st Guards Tank Corps encountered Gollnick's 36.Infanterie-Division (mot.) and were able to overrun an isolated company. However, Ferdinands from schwere Panzerjäger Abteilung 653 arrived to support the division and ambushed the Soviet armour. A single Ferdinand claimed to have knocked out 22 Soviet tanks. The lead elements of 8.Panzer-Division began arriving, and Model agreed to transfer 2.Panzer-Division to reinforce Rendulic.

Schlieben's 18.Panzer-Division was rushed towards the gap created in LIII Armeekorps' front, and ran straight into two tank brigades from Sakhno's 5th Tank Corps north-west of Bolkhov. Schlieben had no support on either flank, and, facing a far superior enemy, could only conduct a mobile delay until reinforcements arrived. Model had instructed Schlieben to halt Bagramyan's armour, not delay it, and was angered to hear that his intent had not been followed. By this point Bagramyan's armour had advanced over 30km from their start line and had created a tactical – but not operational – breakthrough. The Soviet tanks were advancing on backwoods trails, but were avoiding fortified towns.

Greim committed every available air unit to slowing Bagramyan's armour until Model's panzer divisions could arrive to block them. However, Gromov's 1st Air Army proved more competent than either the 15th Air Army or 16th Air Army, and refused to simply cede control of the air to 1.Flieger-Division. Gromov's fighters were able to intercept German close air support missions, shooting down five Bf-110s and fifteen bombers. Overall, Luftflotte 6 lost 38 aircraft to enemy action in one day – more than half of their combat losses during *Zitadelle*. Now Oberkommando der Luftwaffe (OKL) decided to transfer its best fighter unit – III./Jagdgeschwader 52 with Hauptmann Erich Hartmann – to support the defence of the Orel salient. Hitler also finally recognized the importance of unity of command if the Orel salient was to be held, and authorized Model to take command of 2.Panzerarmee as well as his AOK 9.

15 JULY

After several days of reconstituting his units, Rokossovsky's Central Front joined Operation *Kutusov*. Rudenko's 16th Air Army had been rebuilt, and it launched Rokossovsky's offensive with three large-scale attacks against AOK 9's frontline positions. The early termination of *Zitadelle* had left AOK 9 holding a small salient jutting into 13th Army's sector, which was now held by six depleted infantry divisions and 4. and 9. Panzer divisions. Major Sauvant's schwere Panzer-Abteilung 505 remained in the most vulnerable sector, together with 4.Panzer-Division, at Teploye. Rokossovsky launched three attacks against the salient, with the heaviest made by 16th and 19th Tank corps against Teploye. Here Sauvant's Tigers were in an excellent defensive position atop a slight rise, and inflicted heavy losses on the Soviet armour. One Tiger succeeded in knocking out 22 enemy tanks. Despite this success, Model knew that he could not fend off all three Soviet fronts simultaneously, and he began planning tactical withdrawals to shorten his lines.

A German 8cm mortar crew in a concealed position. German defensive tactics were based upon the destructive synergy of automatic weapons, mortars and artillery, which required effective communications. However, once 2.Panzerarmee's front was broken, it was difficult to restore this synergy, and units were more liable to be overwhelmed by Soviet attacks. (Ian Barter)

On Popov's Bryansk Front only Gorbatov's 3rd Army continued to advance, but the arrival of German reinforcements reduced progress to a crawl. Kolpakchi's 63rd Army, with six rifle divisions at the front, was stymied by the still intact 262. Infanterie-Division. By this point the Soviets could advance no further until their artillery was moved forward and effective air support provided. Meanwhile, 20.Panzer-Division reached Bolkhov to stiffen the defence against Bagramyan, while 12. Panzer-Division contained Belov's breakthrough across the Oka. Model was faced with major enemy attacks from north, east and south, and could only respond by repositioning his panzer divisions to try to stem each of the breaches.

It was also becoming apparent that the high tempo of operations demanded by Greim in order to stem the advance of Bagramyan's 11th Guards Army had reduced Luftflotte 6's fuel reserves to a critical level. Both pilots and machines were worn out from 10 days of continuous combat. For the first time, the Luftwaffe's control of the air over the Orel salient began to slip. OKL authorized further transfers to support Luftflotte 6, including Schlachtgeschwader 1 with Hs-129 tank-busters and Hans-Ulrich Rudel's Stukas from III./Sturzkampfgeschwader 2.

16 JULY

Unexpectedly, AOK 9 began withdrawing to its original start lines of 5 July, abandoning Teploye and all other gains. By shortening his front line, Model could pull 9.Panzer-Division out and transfer it northwards, leaving just 4.Panzer-Division and Sauvant's Tigers to reinforce the remaining thin line of infantry. Rokossovsky was apparently caught by surprise by the sudden German withdrawal, and his pursuit was slow. Rudenko's 16th Air Army was able to operate freely over the sector, harassing the German withdrawal.

The arrival of both 2. and 8. Panzer divisions brought the advance of Gorbatov's 3rd Army to a halt along Popov's Bryansk Front. However, Popov began bringing up General-Leytenant Pavel S. Rybalko's 3rd Guards Tank Army; Stavka pushed him to commit it as soon as possible to shatter Rendulic's XXXV Armeekorps once and for all. Since Luftflotte 6 had focused all its resources on stopping the advance of Bagramyam's 11th Guards Army, Naumenko's 15th Air Army was able to regain control of the air over Bryansk Front's lines. It was apparent that Luftflotte 6 could only control one of the three air sectors at a time.

Model sent Harpe to Bolkhov to lead the defence of that key position, Harpe was able to block Bagramyan's armour by using both 18. and 20. Panzer divisions. Luftflotte 6 put all its effort into this sector and

Western Front's offensive, 12–16 July 1943.

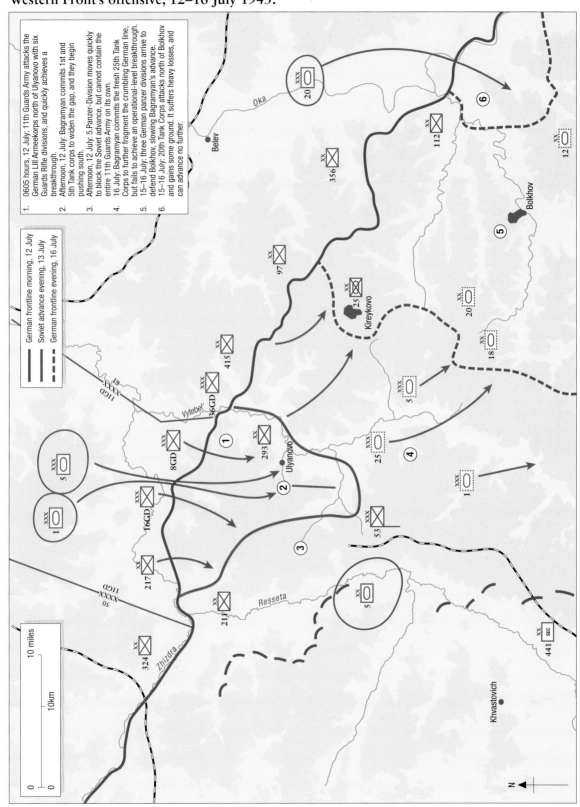

1. 0605 hours, 12 July: 11th Guards Army attacks the German LIII Armeekorps north of Ulyanovo with six Guards Rifle divisions, and quickly achieves a breakthrough.

2. Afternoon, 12 July: Bagramyan commits 1st and 5th Tank corps to widen the gap, and they begin pushing south.

3. Afternoon, 12 July: 5.Panzer-Division moves quickly to block the Soviet advance, but cannot contain the entire 11th Guards Army on its own.

4. 16 July: Bagramyan commits the fresh 25th Tank Corps to further fragment the crumbling German line, but fails to achieve an operational-level breakthrough.

5. 15–16 July: three German panzer divisions arrive to defend Bolkhov, slowing Bagramyan's advance.

6. 15–16 July: 20th Tank Corps attacks north of Bolkhov and gains some ground. It suffers heavy losses, and can advance no further.

German frontline morning, 12 July
Soviet advance evening, 13 July
German frontline evening, 16 July

10 miles
10km
0
0

N

85

After 2.Panzerarmee's front was broken by Operation *Kutusov*, Model was forced to use his armour as a mobile delaying force. Here a PzKpfw IV awaits the Soviets, with its main gun slewed over the back deck. When the Soviets appear on the horizon, it will fire a couple of rounds to destroy the lead vehicle and then race away to the next position. (Süd-Deutsch Zeitung, 26814)

counterattacked with its best units. Soviet anti-aircraft fire was intense here, and even claimed Hans-Ulrich Rudel's Ju-87, which was shot down. Rudel managed to crash-land behind German lines and survived, but other members of his squadron were lost around Bolkhov. Erich Hartmann managed to bag three La-5 fighters in three days around Bolkhov, but this did nothing to alter the fact that the Luftwaffe units were grossly outnumbered. To complicate matters for Gruppe Harpe, Belov's 61st Army committed the fresh 20th Tank Corps into its bridgehead across the Oka, threatening Bolkhov from the east. However, Bagramyan was solely focused on advancing eastwards towards Bolkhov, and failed to send any significant forces south where the German front was wide open and the Orel–Bryansk railway was vulnerable. This was the sole moment during Operation *Kutusov* when the Soviets had an opportunity to encircle at least part of Model's forces. Sokolovsky's situational awareness apparently failed to appreciate this operational opportunity; instead, he single-mindedly pursued tactical objectives. Zhukov also played a hand, in delaying the commitment of Stavka's reserves, which he kept under his personal control.

17 JULY

Model realized that the situation was quickly deteriorating in all three sectors and he decided to launch spoiling attacks with 2. and 8. Panzer divisions to upset Bryansk Front's preparations to renew its offensive. 8.Panzer-Division launched a particularly effective counterattack with its I./Panzer-Regiment 10 that knocked out 25 Soviet tanks. Model also recognized the growing threat to the Orel–Bryansk railway, and he force-marched 9.Panzer-Division towards this area. By the time Bagramyan had begun sending part of 1st Tank Corps south along the Vytebel' River valley, 9.Panzer-Division had already arrived to block them. Despite this temporary success, Gruppe Harpe was still under heavy pressure and was forced to contract its frontline closer to Bolkhov.

Meanwhile, Rokossovsky tried to take advantage of AOK 9's withdrawal and the disappearance of most of the German armour in this sector to launch a hasty attack with Rodin's 2nd Tank Army against 6.Infanterie-Division near Tagino. Once again, Major Sauvant's Tigers proved their worth in repelling enemy armour by knocking out thirty-two T-34 tanks. Although Soviet return fire destroyed two Tigers, Sauvant still had 20 operational Tigers.

18 JULY

Model continued to reposition his forces; if he could stop Bagramyan, the threats in the other sectors would be manageable, he hoped. He sent 10. Panzergrenadier-Division to reinforce Gruppe Harpe at Bolkhov, while Heeresgruppe Mitte agreed to rebuild the battered LIII Armeekorps by transferring 26.Infanterie-Division from AOK 2 and 253.Infanterie-Division from AOK 4. It was hoped that, using these units, the hole in the front could be repaired before Sokolovsky took advantage of it. However, the Soviets had finally recognized that there was a large area with virtually no German forces present, and Bagramyan was ordered to send 11th and 16th Guards Rifle divisions southwards into the void, along with part of 1st Tank Corps. However, Gromov did not re-prioritize his 1st Air Army from close air support of Bagramyan's armour to battlefield interdiction aimed at hindering German reinforcements pouring in by rail; this was a clear mistake. Instead, Bagramyan's and Sokolovsky's tunnel vision focused on Bolkhov, and they committed the fresh 25th Tank Corps to re-energize the push towards the city.

East of Orel, the Germans began to pick up signs that Popov was moving up several new tank corps. Model decided that he could not afford to have his front broken in more than one place at a time, and he ordered XXXV Armeekorps to pull back all along the line, including abandoning the town of Mtensk and the remaining positions on the Zusha River. Other commanders had difficulty getting Hitler and OKH to agree to such common-sense tactical withdrawals; Model simply did it without asking permission. There were no repercussions.

Although Sokolovsky's Western Front – which was essentially fighting with just Bagramyan's 11th Guards Army – was winning the battle, the Soviets failed to seize the opportunity to strike a decisive blow against the German forces in the Orel salient. Popov's Bryansk Front essentially halted for several key days while he brought up his armour and artillery, and Rokossovsky was unwilling to make an all-out effort, even though Model's forces in his sector had very little armour. Offensive action by all three fronts – which was the responsibility of Georgy Zhukov – was poorly coordinated, enabling Model to fight a battle of interior lines. Furthermore, Stavka failed to appreciate that the Germans were stripping other parts of their frontline to reinforce their defences around Orel, and that this offered greater opportunities than merely seizing Bolkhov or Orel. The obvious move – a double envelopment by Rokossovsky shifting Rodin's 2nd Guards Tank Army to attack Roman's XX Armeekorps and Sokolovsky shifting his reserves to overwhelm Jaschke's LV Armeekorps – could have caused a quick collapse of the Orel salient and probable encirclement of at least some German divisions. Stavka, however, proved too conservative in Operation *Kutusov*, opting to push the Germans backwards, rather than striking where they were vulnerable to envelopment.

A group of T-34s manoeuvre rapidly through a ravine. Soviet tankers were beginning to understand how to use cover such as this to approach German defensive positions without suffering crippling losses. Such ravines offered safety from direct fire, but also presented a greater risk of 'throwing track' on uneven ground. (Author's collection)

19 JULY

Although the lead elements of Butkov's 1st Tank Corps reached within 20km of the Bryansk–Orel rail line, 253.Infanterie-Division had already arrived to block them. Both Bagramyan's 11th Guards Army and Belov's 61st Army were now focused on crushing Gruppe Harpe between them and capturing Bolkhov, but Harpe now had four panzer divisions to support his defence. 25th Tank Corps put pressure on 10.Panzergrenadier-Division, but could not break its line. Nevertheless, the German salient at Bolkhov was tenuously held, and under heavy pressure. On Popov's front Rybalko's 3rd Guards Tank Army finally entered the battle, but essentially hit empty positions, since XXXV Armeekorps had already pulled back.

20–25 JULY

Bagramyan's 11th Guards Army had slowed to a crawl due to the arrival of German reinforcements and to the lead units having outrun their supplies. Model shifted the headquarters of XXIII Armeekorps to control the two infantry divisions defending the Orel–Bryansk rail line. OKH even managed to pry the Panzergrenadier-Division Großdeutschland loose from Manstein, now that Heeresgruppe Süd's part of *Zitadelle* was over; this elite formation also was arriving by rail to join XXIII Armeekorps. Zhukov had given Sokolovsky 11th Army, commanded by his protégé General-Leytenant Ivan I. Fedyuninsky, but this powerful formation was committed against the western side of Western Front's breakthrough area, essentially as a flank guard.

Rybalko's 3rd Guards Tank Army finally made its presence felt, and managed to advance almost 20km in a day. However, rather than focusing on a single achievable objective, Popov decided to split Rybalko's armour on two divergent axes. Rybalko's main body, with 15th Tank Corps and 2nd Mechanized Corps, was ordered to advance west to seize Novaya Otrada on the Orel–Mtensk rail line, while 12th Tank Corps was ordered to swing southwards to strike 262. Infanterie-Division's flank, in order to enable 63rd Army to advance. While this decision enabled Popov's forces to conduct a 'broad front' advance towards Orel, it deprived his primary exploitation force of the mass it needed to achieve a decisive breakthrough.

A German Marder III tank destroyer awaits Soviet armour during the fighting around Orel in early August 1943. Model's hopes for pulling off a defensive masterpiece at Orel – like he did against Zhukov's Operation *Mars* in the Rzhev salient – were frustrated by the German Army's increasing inability to sustain a protracted high-intensity battle. The only option became delay and withdrawal to the Hagen Stellung. (Author's collection)

Over the next several days the Soviets gradually closed in on Gruppe Harpe at Bolkhov. Although Belov's 61st Army was able to reach its outskirts by 25 July, Harpe had deployed a ring of steel around the town. In Popov's sector Rybalko's armour was too dispersed to seize Orel, which was now defended by 12.Panzer-Division. Popov's rifle divisions managed to gain some ground, but the German defences around Orel were firming up. Unable to mount a successful frontal assault on Orel, Popov decided to shift all of Rybalko's 3rd Guards Tank Army into the 63rd Army sector, to create a breach south-east of Orel, in conjunction with Rokossovsky's forces.

26 JULY

For the first time during Operation *Kutusov*, the Soviets were able to attack with two fronts against a single portion of the German line – the boundary between Rendulic's XXXV Armeekorps and Zorn's XXXXVI Panzerkorps. Rybalko's 3rd Guards Tank Army struck 292.Infanterie-Division south of Ore; surprisingly it suffered heavy losses and failed to achieve a breakthrough. Rokossovsky had more luck in his sector, where XXXXVI Panzerkorps had been stretched to cover the entire front formerly held by four corps. With only 4.Panzer-Division in tactical reserve, Zorn could not prevent 13th, 48th and 70th armies from shoving his depleted divisions backwards, and he was forced to give ground. The town of Zmiyevka was abandoned.

After days of positional warfare in Bagramyan's sector, Zhukov finally released General-Leytenant Vasily M. Badanov's 4th Guards Tank Army and General-Leytenant Vladimir V. Kriukov's 2nd Guards Cavalry Corps to re-energize Sokolovsky's offensive. When the Luftwaffe detected the approach of this mass of manoeuvre, Model realized that it was time to abandon Bolkhov and contract his forces to hold onto Orel for as long as possible.

27 JULY–3 AUGUST

Over the course of the next several days, Model was able to stabilize the front around Orel and inflict heavy losses upon Popov's Bryansk Front. Rybalko's 3rd Guards Tank Army had lost 669 tanks after just a week of combat and had to be pulled out of action to reconstitute. Frießner's XXIII Armeekorps was able to form a viable defensive line north of the Orel–Bryansk rail line, centred on the Panzergrenadier-Division Großdeutschland, which had arrived just in the nick of time. Sokolovsky had committed Kriukov's 2nd Guards Cavalry Corps to reach the rail line, but the door was now shut. A great opportunity had been squandered by the Red Army.

From this point on the Germans had regained a continuous front all around the Orel salient, and the Soviet armies simply began pressing in from all sides. Model was able to inflict heavy losses upon the Soviet units closing in upon Orel, but even though he now had 8 of the German Army's 16 panzer divisions, he could not stop them. Nor could he stop the endless barrage of artillery and air strikes that hammered his retreating forces. Model's priority now shifted to saving as much as possible, particularly the 20,000 German wounded in Orel's hospitals and the 53,000 tons of supplies in its depots. He raised the idea of evacuating the Orel salient with Hitler, but couched it in terms of an organized withdrawal to the Hagen Stellung that would release panzer divisions for counterattacks elsewhere. On 31 July Hitler agreed to let Model evacuate the Orel salient, which went into effect the next day as Operation *Herbstreise*. Heavy rain hindered the evacuation, and the roads heading west out of Orel were crammed with vehicles, inviting air attack.

A German PzKpfw IV tank commander scans for the enemy at the edge of Orel. 12.Panzer-Division was picked to form a rearguard to delay the Soviet entrance into the city while the rest of AOK 9 retreated across the Oka River bridges. (Süd-Deutsch Zeitung, 10600)

Soviet attacks intensified as they noticed the Germans begin withdrawing. On 2 August a Soviet air strike killed Zorn, the commander of XXXXVI Panzerkorps, near Kromy. Gruppe Harpe fell back quickly toward Karachev on the Orel–Bryansk rail line, with Badanov's 4th Guards Tank Army in pursuit. Frießner's XXIII Armeekorps established a strong defence anchored on Karachev, which gave the retreating German forces a place of refuge. XXXXVI and XXXXVII Panzerkorps continued to delay Rokossovsky's three armies, mostly with just infantry and some assault guns.

Soviet T-34s attack, with infantry close behind. Western and Bryansk fronts hammered repeatedly at Model's forward troops, suffering very heavy losses in the process. However, Heeresgruppe Mitte lacked the resources to sustain this battle of attrition and was forced to gradually withdraw from the Orel salient. (Author's collection)

Soldiers from Bryansk Front's 380th Rifle Division raise the flag of liberation over Orel on the morning of 5 August 1943, just a month after *Zitadelle* began. Recovering the city cost the Red Army the exorbitant price of over 400,000 casualties. (Author's collection)

4–5 AUGUST

Model remained in Orel with a skeleton staff and personally supervised the rearguard action conducted by 12.Panzer-Division. Hitler was worried that the Soviets would capture the bridges over the Oka River in the city and use them to push their armour across, so he demanded that Model immediately destroy the bridges – even though the German rearguards were on the other side of the river. Model simply ignored him and waited for the last vehicles of 12.Panzer-Division to cross before blowing up the bridges. Much of Orel was on fire as the Germans withdrew westward. The next morning troops from Kolpakchi's 63rd Army liberated the smouldering city.

6–18 AUGUST

The Soviets continued to pursue Model's forces as they withdrew to the Hagen Stellung. Rodin's 2nd Tank Army and 70th Army mounted strong attacks against Lemelsen's XXXXVII Panzerkorps, which threatened to overwhelm his weakened infantry divisions. 4.Panzer-Division served as rearguard, fending off jabs by Rodin's tankers, until the infantry divisions could withdraw. Gruppe Harpe took over the defence of Karachev in the centre of the shrinking salient, preserving German lines of communications. The wave of Soviet armour and infantry continued pushing westwards, overrunning Karachev on 14 August. However, the three Soviet fronts were exhausted after weeks of heavy fighting. By evacuating the salient Model had significantly shortened his frontline, falling back on prepared positions in the Hagen Stellung. On 18 August Stavka recognized that Western, Bryansk and Central fronts needed to stop and replace losses. Operation *Kutusov* was thus ended.

AFTERMATH

AOK 9 achieved nothing of operational value during Operation *Zitadelle*, which cost it 22,201 casualties and 71 armoured fighting vehicles destroyed. Although a number of accounts have attempted to play up the extent of 'massive tank battles' on the northern front of the Kursk salient, the action in this sector was dominated by mine warfare, artillery and air attacks. In contrast to the short-lived *Zitadelle*, the 38-day Operation *Kutusov* achieved significant operational results by forcing the Germans to abandon the Orel salient. Moreover, it cost them far greater casualties: 88,000 in total, of which 27,000 were dead or missing. Losses of armour were also much heavier during *Kutusov*, with at least 229 tanks and tank destroyers destroyed, plus hundreds more damaged. Most of the eight panzer divisions involved in stopping *Kutusov* suffered heavy losses in men and materiel. Altogether, Heeresgruppe Mitte lost one-third of its available armour in July 1943 – a grievous loss for no gain.

Model's AOK 9 never had the opportunity to approach Kursk, and it does not appear that a serious effort was made to reach this distant objective. Instead, AOK 9 settled on trying to seize some tactical objectives and then hoped to win a battle of attrition with a much stronger opponent. German offensive tactics used during *Zitadelle* were frequently faulty, with poor coordination between infantry, panzers and artillery. Units like 2.Panzer-Division often moved hither and yon, wasting considerable time. After *Zitadelle* had ended, a German regimental commander noted that many of his replacement troops were inadequately trained for this kind of high-intensity warfare, and that morale began to plummet as the troops realized that their losses could not be replaced – in contrast to those of the Soviets. While none of Model's units were entirely destroyed in the battle, his infantry units would never regain their full effectiveness and his armoured strength was much reduced by the time that Orel fell. In terms of weaponry, the Ferdinands performed poorly in the breakthrough role, but they and the Tigers were well suited to the defensive role. In particular, the Germans claimed that schwere Panzerjäger-Regiment 656 knocked out 502 enemy tanks between 5 and 27 July, while it lost 39 out of 90 Ferdinands.

The Red Army's performance on the northern front had mixed results. Rokossovsky made few mistakes in the entire campaign and he fought a cautious defensive battle during both *Zitadelle* and *Kutusov*. Soviet defensive tactics were much improved. Although Rokossovsky failed to 'impale' Model's army on his defences, he did prevent Model from seizing any objectives of real tactical value or destroying any of Central Front's

The victors: tankers from Rodin's 2nd Tank Army. (Author's collection)

formations. Sokolovsky had also fought too conservative a battle during *Kutusov* and squandered his chance to cut Model's lines of communications before he could transfer units. Popov's battle management was the poorest, and his front suffered some of the heaviest losses for it. Altogether, the Soviet Central, Western and Bryansk fronts suffered a total of 429,890 casualties during *Kutusov*. When added to the losses during *Zitadelle*, the Red Army lost a total of over 463,000 casualties in seven weeks of combat on the northern front. In contrast to the loss of *c.* 220 tanks during *Zitadelle*, the three Soviet fronts lost a total of 2,586 tanks during *Kutusov*. Thus the standard historiography of the battle of Kursk, which sees *Zitadelle* as the main event, is incorrect insofar as the northern front is concerned – it was merely the prelude to the Red Army achieving clear battlefield superiority over Heeresgruppe Mitte.

THE BATTLEFIELD TODAY

Virtually all of the 'battlefield tourism' associated with the battle of Kursk revolves around Prokhorovka and the southern sector of the battle, with very little attention devoted to the northern battlefields. Indeed, the nearest major international airport to the northern front is in Belgorod, nearly 300km to the south. Yet the Russians are aware of their past and have made efforts in recent years to mark the sacrifices made on the northern front. Anyone seeking to tour the northern front should plan on making Orel their base of operations, even though it lacks an international airport. While Orel Yuzhny Airport (OEL) mostly serves domestic flights, the city is a transportation hub that is large enough to offer proper hotels, restaurants, car rental facilities and tour guides.

In Orel there is a fairly modern Military History Museum on Normandiya-Neman Street that has some displays and weapons related to the northern sector in the battle of Kursk, including artifacts recovered by modern excavation. The museum also boasts a full-scale diorama of a World War II trench and several other immersive-type displays. However, the Orel Military History Museum covers a broad swathe of history going back to the 17th century and is not focused merely on World War II. Oddly, the museum also has a number of post-World War 2 US-made weapons on display, and hosts re-enactor groups depicting modern US Special Forces in Afghanistan, so the purpose of this museum might not exactly suit foreign tourists. Perhaps the best museum-type displays that actually cover the fighting on the northern front are located in the Taginskoy High School in Glazunovka, which runs a virtual history project on the battle.

In the town of Ponyri, with boasts a current population of 11,000, a memorial complex known as the 'Heroes of the North Face of the Kursk Bulge' was opened in July 2013 to commemorate the 70th anniversary of the battle. It has the usual outdoor collection of Soviet artillery pieces and granite markers depicting Soviet war heroes. There is also the obligatory tank mounted on a victory plinth – a T-34/85, which was not actually in service during the battle. Ponyri also has a historical museum, which does focus on the fighting around the town. However, Ponyri is still a sleepy, agricultural place, with rusting statues of Lenin still standing, and is not well suited to handling foreign tourists. Teploye is currently a cluster of about 30 houses, surrounded by acres of farmland, but in 2011 the Russian Federation finally got around to erecting a memorial grotto to mark the 1943 fighting around the town. As usual, the Russian choice of weapons to mark a battlefield has little or no connection to the actual equipment used; in this location, an IS-2 heavy tank sits atop the plinth near Teploye. Further east, modern Ol'khovatka is about three times the size of Teploye, but only has a large Red Star to mark the site of the fighting north of the town. Kursk's northern battlefields remain part of the 'undiscovered' part of World War II on the Eastern Front, beyond the bounds of the normal interpretation of the battle. Yet thousands of lives were lost on this ground in July 1943, which identify this as a battlefield worth remembering in its own right.

FURTHER READING

Bergström, C., *Kursk: The Air Battle, July 1943*, Ian Allan Publishing: Hersham, 2007

Bukeikhanov, P., *Kurskaya bitva, Oborona: Planirovaniye i podgotovka opyeratsii 'Tsitadyel'' 1943*, Tsentrpoligraf: Moscow, 2011

Glantz, D.M., *Soviet Defensive Tactics at Kursk, July 1943*, Combat Studies Institute Report No. 11: Fort Leavenworth, KS, 1986

Glantz, D.M. and House, J.M., *The Battle of Kursk*, University Press of Kansas: Lawrence, KS, 1999

Münch, K-H., *The Combat History of German Heavy Anti-Tank Unit 653 in World War II*, Stackpole Books: Mechanicsburg, PA, 2005

Newton, S.H. (ed.), *Kursk: The German View*, Da Capo Press: Cambridge, MA, 2002

Rendulic, L., *Gekämpft, gesiegt, geschlagen*, Welsermühl Verlag: Heidelberg, 1952

Rokossovsky, *K., Soldatskiy Dolg*, Military Publishing: Moscow, 1988

Shchekotikhin, E., *Krupneishee tankovoe srazhenie Velikoi Otechestvennoi: Bitva za Orel*, EKSMO: Moscow, 2009

Zetterling, N. and Frankson, A., *Kursk 1943: A Statistical Analysis*, Frank Cass: London, 2000

INDEX